Why Customers Don't Do What You Want Them to Do— And What to Do About It

Other McGraw-Hill Books by Ferdinand F. Fournies

COACHING FOR IMPROVED WORK PERFORMANCE

WHY EMPLOYEES DON'T DO WHAT THEY'RE SUPPOSED TO DO—
AND WHAT TO DO ABOUT IT

Why Customers Don't Do What You Want Them to Do— And What to Do About It

Ferdinand F. Fournies

McGraw-Hill, Inc.

New York   San Francisco   Washington, D.C.   Auckland   Bogotá
Caracas   Lisbon   London   Madrid   Mexico City   Milan
Montreal   New Delhi   San Juan   Singapore
Sydney   Tokyo   Toronto

Library of Congress Cataloging-in-Publication Data

Fournies, Ferdinand F.
    Why customers don't do what you want them to do and what to do
about it / Ferdinand F. Fournies.
        p.   cm.
    Includes index.
    ISBN 0-07-021700-9 (hc. : acid-free paper) :   —ISBN
0-07-021701-7 (pbk. : acid-free paper) :
    1. Sales personnel—Training of.   2. Sales management.
3. Selling.   I. Title.
HF5439.8.F68   1994
658.8′1—dc20   93-22717
                                                          CIP

1 2 3 4 5 6 7 8 9 0   DOC/DOC   9 9 8 7 6 5 4 3

ISBN 0-07-021700-9 (hc.)
ISBN 0-07-021701-7 (pbk.)

*The sponsoring editor for this book was David Conti, the editing supervisor
was Jane Palmieri, and the production supervisor was Donald Schmidt. It was
set in Palatino by McGraw-Hill's Professional Book Group composition unit.*

Printed and bound by R. R. Donnelley & Sons Company.

This book is printed on recycled, acid-free paper
containing a minimum of 50% recycled de-inked fiber.

To Betty
my friend, my partner, my wife

About the Author

Ferdinand F. Fournies is the best-selling author of *Why Employees Don't Do What They're Supposed to Do—And What to Do About It* and *Coaching for Improved Work Performance*. Both books have been translated and read around the world. An expert in management techniques and sales training, Fournies presents seminars around the world and consults with international clients such as Merck, Eastman Kodak, American Cyanamid, Hewlett-Packard, 3M, and Prudential.

Contents

Preface

Back around the turn of the century it was popular to characterize selling as an art because psychology was a budding science, and we had not yet developed the skills to analyze human interactions as a cause-effect relationship. It was enough to implore salespeople to "know your product, know your customers, and cover your territory." When analyzing a salesperson's failure, it seemed adequate to describe him or her as "not having that killer instinct," or "not hungry enough," or "just not having what it takes to be in sales." The common belief was that salespeople are born, not made, implying that successful salespeople had personal qualities or instincts genetically derived which caused them to be successful. There was little understanding of how selling worked, and no one could describe exactly how to do it, so it was obviously an art, or perhaps even trickery.

But because selling was such a critical part of any business's success, it became the subject of intense analysis to answer the question, "What do successful salespeople do differently than do unsuccessful salespeople?" That analysis over the last almost 100 years has revealed unequivocally that selling is a collection of interventions anyone can use and if done correctly will lead to sales success.

Although we have learned a lot about selling to date, not every company has accessed that knowledge. For example, until recently selling was a dirty word in the banking industry and still is in some banks. I've had banking clients tell me, "We don't sell. We do account development." When I ask, "What is that?" they tell me, "Selected employees will contact doctors, lawyers, and other investors for the purpose of getting their money as deposits." But everything they describe in their account development activities is, in fact, selling. Because they are hung up on their abhorrence of "selling," they cut themselves off from the vast amount of available knowledge which would help them achieve their goal.

Public accounting firms have the same problem. One client was telling me that one of the key ingredients for becoming a partner in his public accounting firm was to be able to develop accounts. He said that unfortunately at times a potential partner would have all the other qualities that would make a good partner except that the person could not develop accounts. Therefore, the firm would not promote that person, and usually he or she would resign. When I asked what developing accounts meant, everything he told me described selling activities to get more business. He was quite chagrined when I pointed out that what he called developing accounts was actually selling and if his firm had sent the potential partner to school to learn how to sell, it would not have had to go through the loss of that high-quality person.

Recently I was conducting a sales skills seminar for a major railroad whose salespeople had little or no previous sales training. When I was finished with the seminar, a marketing director expressed his amazement that the things a person could do in selling were so specific and could have such dramatic effect on customers. He said, "I didn't know that selling could be analyzed so scientifically."

Situational analysis has brought us to the point where we are now able to write down everything a customer could say or do in a specific selling situation. We can also write down everything the salesperson should say or do in that selling situation to either cause the customer to say or to do something or counteract what the customer has said or done, with the ultimate goal of making the sale.

However, companies vary widely in how they access available sales knowledge, and there is even wide variation in performance among salespeople in the same company selling the same product. In most companies, usually a small percentage of salespeople are selling above 100 percent of target or quota, a majority of salespeople are selling slightly below the target or quota, and a small percentage are 70 percent below quota. All these salespeople sell the same product to the same kind of customers and have been through the same sales training program. This variation in sales performance is frustrating for most sales managers, and the tendency is to blame it on a bad hiring decision. But when we travel with these salespeople as consultants observing how they sell, the reason for the performance difference is not a mystery; the successful salespeople do certain things differently from the unsuccessful salespeople.

One consistent major difference we have found is that successful salespeople seem to concentrate on helping customers to buy versus merely selling the product. They certainly want the sale as badly as any other salesperson, but their way of getting it is to focus on helping the customer to buy. They didn't learn this in sales training, and many of them are unaware that they are doing it. In contrast, the unsuccessful salespeople focus solely on selling the product and become frustrated because they are getting fewer sales. Some salespeople focus so intently on "selling" when presenting their product that they don't give the customer a chance to participate and even interrupt the customer when he or she tries to participate. It is difficult to break this habit, especially if the salesperson has several years of experience.

During my 20 years of consulting experience in training sales managers, designing sales training programs, and teaching sales skills, it has become quite evident that if unsuccessful salespeople start doing the same things as the successful salespeople do, they will be equally successful. I have discovered a breakthrough concept that has helped salespeople become more successful, and that concept is redefining the selling process as "selling is the management of buying." This breakthrough idea is the understanding that salespeople do "selling things" and customers do "buying things," therefore the only purpose of a salesperson doing selling things is to get the customer to do buying things. As simple as it sounds, this understanding totally switches the emphasis of selling activities to more resemble what successful salespeople do, which is to help people to buy. In practice this single redefinition of the selling job has been the pivot point that has helped salespeople change from being mediocre to being highly successful.

The purpose of this book is to recast selling according to that definition, to help all salespeople understand how to change their emphasis or focus from selling to helping people to buy. But to successfully *manage the buying*, it is essential that salespeople have a detailed understanding of the customer's world from the customer's point of view. As pointed out later in the book, customers don't do dumb things on purpose; everything they do seems like a good idea to them at that time. It is only the salesperson's lack of understanding that makes the customer appear dumb. So the majority of this book concentrates on helping salespeople to understand each selling situation from the customer's point of view. I've used situation analysis in presenting 24 common customer situations every salesperson faces as selling obstacles. Each situation is followed by specific solutions (172 in all) a salesperson can use to understand and overcome those common obstacles that vary from the earliest one of "I can't get an appointment" to the last one of "he won't buy my product." The book concentrates on helping salespeople get past those obstacles or "critical moments" when the success of the sale rests on the salesperson's ability to do the right thing at the right time.

If you are new to selling, you have no bad habits to eliminate, and this book will give you an in-depth understanding of the customer you will not find anywhere else. If you are an experienced salesperson, this book will help you orient your sales skills to more effectively *manage the buying process*. You will be introduced to new concepts and techniques you can use as "selling is the management of buying." You will discover the six key differences between "professionals" and the "also-rans" of the world, and you will learn how to use these keys to build your own success. You will become sensitive to the critical "moments of truth" in selling when you can unknowingly win or lose the sale, and you will learn how to increase your control of each selling situation. You will learn how to maximize your selling time investment to bring you more sales per selling minute, and you will be able to apply critical analysis to each selling situation both to avoid repeating failures and to replicate success, which will give you continuous improvement.

My objective in this book is to drastically change your sales approach from "selling" to "helping people to buy." At a time when everyone accepts the fact that the buyer is ultimately the most important person to business, this is the most effective approach to selling.

Ferdinand F. Fournies

The Last
Exciting Job

Selling for a living is one of the last exciting jobs left in modern society which embraces those elements normally found in adventures such as climbing mountains, setting deep-sea diving records, and exploring uncharted lands. In those adventures, an essential element for success is a person's ability to perform certain critical skills perfectly, whether working alone or as part of a team. The individual is confronted with what you could call "moments of truth," when success or failure hinges on the person's decision and skill at that critical moment: Do I go left or right into the rapids? Do I stand still in front of the bear or run? Do I camp now on the rock face and assume the weather will hold, or do I climb in the dark? Do I explore the underwater cavern alone now or come back next year and do it with a team? Adventures also require detailed planning, organization, and practice to prepare individuals for those critical moments of truth—when success depends on doing the right thing at the right time. All these aspects of an adventure can be found in the selling job.

I am not implying that a salesperson is some kind of independent soldier of fortune or "fast gun" roaming the territories looking for a challenge. Most salespeople are not self-employed and do not work totally alone. In most companies, salespeople get a lot of support from their research, manufacturing, financial, marketing, and customer service departments. But no matter how much company support you have as a salesperson, there comes the moment of truth when you, like the bullfighter, stand alone. You are the only one facing the customer, and you will win or lose the sale according to how you perform at that critical moment.

In selling, as in exploring, you don't get rewarded for efforts; you get rewarded only for success. Most jobs in business are not like that; people work all day and get paid for performance, with little or no daily measurement of results. In most jobs, it is difficult to measure results, because one person rarely does any job from beginning to end. Any project or piece of work is touched by many people along the way, and rarely do any of them see the completed process. In some jobs a good result is getting everything from the in-basket into the out-basket; there are no critical moments and not much winning or losing in a day's work. In contrast, the selling day is filled with winning and losing. Merely getting appointments with customers is a contest, and just beating the traffic to keep each appointment on time is a challenge. Each customer contact is a contest to get him or her to tell you what you need to know. Presenting your product and overcoming the many obstacles to getting the sale is a contest. There is a definite thrill in walking away from a customer with the sales order in your hand. It is similar to finally getting to the mountaintop and feeling "I made it."

But the reality of adventures is that not every moment of every day of an adventure is filled with thrilling and critical moments. There is a lot of boring routine that must be repeated, and things don't always go smoothly. There are delays, disappointments, obstacles to overcome, bad weather, equipment failure, injuries. The reality of selling is that there also are disappointments and obstacles; you don't get a "yes" from every customer. It takes personal maturity and professionalism to bounce back from a "no" from one customer at 10 o'clock in the morning and smile at the customer you see at 10:30.

In most jobs people drive the same route to the same building to work with the same people every day. They are surrounded by familiarity. An outside salesperson may drive to different places each day, meeting strangers and trying to get them to do things they didn't plan to do—oftentimes things they may not want to do, even though they need to—and get them to spend money to do it. In most jobs, if you look up from your work, you will be reassured by seeing your fellow workers and even your boss. In most selling jobs, if you look up from your work, you see only customers and strangers. In some outside selling jobs, you may see your boss only once a month. I don't mean to imply that nonselling jobs are unimportant or are performed by drones. I am merely pointing out some important differences between most selling jobs and most other jobs.

Even some of the terms describing certain selling activities characterize the unusual aspects of the selling job. For example, the term *prospecting* is used to describe the activity of searching for and qualifying individuals who have a potential for eventually becoming a customer. The term *missionary work* describes the general activity of contacting people who know nothing about your product for the purpose of familiarizing them with your company and your product or services. Both of these activities are conducted predominantly with strangers. This does not mean that salespeople never see the same person twice or that salespeople don't have customers who eventually become friends. That varies depending upon the nature of the sales-call pattern required to sell any particular product. If you sell products that are purchased after one or two sales calls and that are not repeat sales items, you will not be seeing many familiar faces each day. Nevertheless, you have to perform at your best in unfamiliar and sometimes unfriendly surroundings. Selling can be a lonely job, but not as lonely as shivering in your sleeping bag in a snowstorm hanging on the side of a mountain at 14,000 feet.

Just as not everyone can be a successful explorer or mountain climber, not everyone can be a successful salesperson. I am not referring to that old sobriquet, "Salespeople are born, not made." That is nonsense. It would be just as silly to say golfers are born, not made. What I mean is that successful selling requires professionalism, study, self-discipline, and a lot of hard work. There are people who can't or don't want to exert the extra effort required to do that. This is the same reason why everyone does not climb the highest mountains or compete in the Olympics.

It's "Show Business"

If you have ever been in the audience of a stage play or rock concert, you probably assumed that the actors or the musicians were having as much fun as you were. That is a common misunderstanding by people who are not entertainers. You see, when you are watching a stage play, you are acting normally—you are enjoying yourself. The actors are not acting normally; they are playing roles so you will enjoy yourself. At rock concerts, when musicians play music they have played hundreds of times already, their fun is less related to the enjoyment in playing music than it is to the things they are talking about on stage, such as who made what mistake and how weird the audience is. Some musicians who play well together are combative and do not talk to each other off stage.

To put it in perspective, you can ask yourself, "How come they are perspiring and I am not?" The answer is, "They are working to entertain you, and you are being entertained." It would never occur to entertainers that they are performing to enjoy themselves. I'm not saying that entertainers don't find enjoyment from doing something well or from getting a positive audience response. But it would never occur to entertainers that the purpose of their performance is to enjoy themselves. Their lack of enjoyment or boredom will increase according to how many times the same performance is repeated.

Picture yourself sitting in the audience of a theater and you are about to see the 5087th performance of a famous musical show. But before the curtain rises, one of the actors appears on stage and says, "Ladies and Gentlemen, we've done this show 5086 times and we are a little bored. So tonight we are going to do something different. The members of the cast will do some acrobatics, and I have been taking lessons in sleight of hand, so I will do some card tricks and saw one of the stagehands in half. We know it's not the show you've come to see, but we, the cast, will have more fun this evening." After you hear that, would you sit there and be satisfied or would you jump to your feet and yell, "I want to see the regular show"? The point is that no matter how many shows the actors have performed before today, you have not seen the show yet. So if the actors do not do the 5087th performance tonight, you will not see that particular show tonight.

The critical point of understanding from the actor's point of view is that no matter how many stage shows you have done as an actor, the show you do tonight stands by itself. It is not influenced by how good or bad the previous shows were or how good or bad future shows will be. If you don't do this show today, the audience will not see it. And if you perform badly, they will see a bad show.

This same element of show business applies to selling situations. Picture yourself as a salesperson who has presented your product to five separate customers so far today. By the time you get to the sixth customer, it is 4 o'clock in the afternoon, you are tired, you are hot, and your bag of selling materials is getting heavy. So you say to the customer, "I left my product samples and other selling materials in the car because I am tired of carrying them. But here's the phone number of Mr. Smith whom I called on this morning at 9 o'clock when the weather was cooler and I was not tired. You don't know who he is, but please call him on the phone now and ask him to tell you what a great sales presentation I gave him."

Obviously, to make such a suggestion to the customer would be stupid. If you intend to present your product to six customers today and you only present it to five customers, the sixth customer doesn't get to see your product. Just as in show business, your previous good and bad presentations, as well as your future presentations to different customers, are not relevant to the sixth customer; he or she doesn't get to see the show.

You Can't Go Wrong Copying the Winners

Not too long ago, as part of a consulting assignment with an insurance company, I was traveling with a salesperson to observe that company's selling techniques. The sales manager had told me that the company provided salespeople with scripts of specific words to use when describing certain aspects of their product. These scripts were developed as a result of a detailed analysis of the difference in techniques used by their effective and ineffective salespeople. The ultimate conclusion was that the most effective salespeople said things in more effective ways than the unsuccessful salespeople, and so the company created word-for-word questions and answers for salespeople to use in creating their sales presentation. The scripts did not prescribe everything a salesperson should say as in a canned presentation, but they presented the most effective way of asking and answering critical questions.

Throughout the day I noticed that this salesperson changed the way he talked about the product with each customer, although he was talking about the same product each time. He never said the same thing twice. At the end of the day, I mentioned that I was aware that the company provided detailed scripts of presentations which salespeople were expected to follow when describing certain aspects of the product. Then I said, "I noticed that you changed what you said to each customer today although you were describing the same features and benefits. I wonder why." His response was, "I feel like a robot when I say the same thing every time. I want to have a little more freedom and flexibility out here instead of acting like a dummy saying the same thing every time." I then asked him if he thought that Sir Lawrence Olivier felt like a dummy or a robot after doing Shakespeare's *Othello* for 30 years. His response was, "That's different. You have to be more creative in selling."

I proceeded to explain to him that it's not different, and that you don't have to be more creative unless what you plan to do will not work for that customer. In selling as in show business and even in humor, the primary vehicle is speech: the words you use. If you intend to tell a funny story and you change the words, nobody will laugh. The story is only funny if you tell it in a funny way. When an actor plays a Shakespearean role for 30 years, he does not change the words; he just tries to deliver them better each time. The same thing applies in selling. If you or your organization has discovered the most effective words to describe the features and benefits of your product, or the most effective words to use to get a customer to describe his or her needs, or to buy your product, and you do not use the same words, you are not using the most effective way.

Practice Does Make Perfect

One time when vacationing in Atlantic City, I noticed on the boardwalk a man standing behind a raised podium selling glass cutters. I stopped to listen to his presentation because I, like most people who occasionally try to cut glass, do it badly; for every three pieces I cut, one is usable. His presentation lasted a full 20 minutes and included actual glass-cutting demonstrations. His story was interesting. He described the problems and hazards of cutting glass and made some reference to the history of glassmaking, as well as pointing out the design attributes of the particular hand-held glass cutter that he was hawking. And while he was talking, without interruption, he wielded his glass cutter like a razor cutting paper. Apparently without much care, he cut curves and angles and half moons and made a lot of big pieces into smaller pieces. By the time he was finished, he had 15 to 20 people standing around watching him, and most of us bought a glass cutter. His presentation got a lot of attention because he was telling an interesting story; it had a beginning, a middle, and an ending, like all good sales presentations.

For the next several days when walking up and down the boardwalk, I passed the same man hawking his glass cutter at least 10 times, and each time he held the attention of his small audience. What impressed me the most was that each time I heard him speak, he was saying exactly the same words but with as much interest and emphasis and flourish as though it were the first time he was doing it. He gathered his audience, held their attention, and got them to buy his product because he romanticized his product. It was not just the words he used: he smiled; he frowned; he showed his teeth; he leaned forward; he modulated his voice; he demonstrated excitement about what he was doing. He was making it look easy and interesting and not at all boring because he was acting. That was quite a feat considering the many 20-minute presentations he made in 3 hours each evening. But the real kicker was on the third day when a different man was selling the glass cutter. I listened to his entire presentation and was amazed that he said and did everything exactly the same as the first salesman and was equally successful.

Another fine point of show business that is frequently missed by people unfamiliar with it is that there is a tremendous amount of preparation and practice before a show is ready to be presented to the public. This painstaking rehearsal ensures that the theatrical characters appear to be real and the concert music appears to be spontaneous and thrilling. When actors flub their lines or are out of position on stage, or the musicians deviate from what was practiced, you will see a performance that is less than perfect and less than thrilling. These same elements of show business are also in selling.

You can't decide whether show business is or is not a part of selling; it is there whether you like it or not. Your only choice is whether to pay attention to it and use it for your own success. You have to develop the most effective ways of asking your questions, or answering the questions customers ask. You have to learn how to hold your product and your advertising literature so that you do it with ease and style to romanticize your product. You have to learn how to modulate your voice and tone quality and use smiles, facial expressions, and body movements to emphasize the excitement and interest you want your customer to feel about your products. And you have to understand that this will not come naturally—you have to work at it. Unfortunately, the more sales presentations you make in any particular day, the greater the likelihood that what you're doing will become boring and you will tend to do less and less acting each time. You have to resist that.

Accept the fact that each sales presentation to a customer is like a show or a concert and you may not get a second chance with that customer. Therefore, it's okay to feel tired or hot or bored before the call, and it's okay to feel tired or hot or maybe even disappointed after the call if you were not successful. But when you approach the next customer, you must say to yourself, "I hear the overture beginning. The house lights are dimming. It's time for me to go on stage. The curtain is rising. The show must go on." You are going on stage—you have to get your act together.

PART 1

Three Keys to Your Sales Success

1

How to Be a Professional Instead of an Also-Ran

The term *professionalism* is one of those words that are heard frequently as a part of our daily life and that are obviously used too loosely. I have heard some people described as professional troublemakers or professional goof-offs. In the movies characters are referred to as professional hit men and professional lawmen. I've heard sales managers when describing individual salespeople say "she's very professional" or that "he's not very professional." I think of my family physician as a professional although he never said that he is one. I know lawyers consider themselves as professionals, but is a paralegal also a professional? Recently I had an addition put on my house by a man who said he was a professional builder, but after he was finished, I was sure he was not one. When displaying my wood carvings at craft fairs, people ask me if I am a professional wood-carver, and I say no, wood carving is only my hobby. I started to seriously question the meaning of the term *professional* when the limousine driver I use traveling to the airport told me that he was a professional limousine driver. This is the same person who has called to cancel trips because of snow, who can't find me at airports, and who occasionally shows up late.

The Hidden Differences
That Make a Professional

The obvious questions are "What is a professional?" and "How do you get to be one?" Are you a professional only because you have acquired certain educational degrees and certificates? Does someone have to give you that title, or can you give the title to yourself merely by saying, "I am a professional"? To answer these questions, I started analyzing the differences between the way so-called professionals do things in life as compared with everyone else. The differences I found were quite revealing as follows.

Difference 1. Professionals Do
What They Do Better Than
Almost Everybody Else

Whether their field is sports, medicine, plumbing, or acting, professionals perform to perfection. Frequently they appear to perform without effort, but they demonstrate an expertise that is enviable. Professionals perform at a level of perfection rarely obtained by others and frequently do things the "also-rans" in the world believe cannot be done. Although they don't say it out loud, professionals seem to follow the very old rule, "If it's worth doing, it's worth doing well." Their outstanding performance can probably be attributed to the next two items.

Difference 2. Professionals
Know More About What
They Are Doing Than
Everybody Else

This was an easy conclusion to come to in comparing the difference between what my doctor knows about my health and what I know about my health; or what my lawyer knows about contracts and what I know about contracts. They both went to college to acquire all that useful knowledge. But getting a college degree is not what is important; it's the "knowing" that counts. For example, a person can know more than most people about wood carving or plumbing or computers or dancing or selling and qualify under this requirement. The "knowing" relates to the detailed understanding of all the nuances of the subject.

Difference 3. Professionals Are Always Trying to Improve

The clear difference here is that the also-rans look in the mirror and tell themselves, "You're great," but professionals look in the mirror and say, "You could be better." You can call that a difference in personal drive or attitude or motivation, but the labels are not important. What is important is that professionals seem to exert a continuous effort to learn more and practice more in order to get better at what they are doing. When you compliment outstanding performers for how wonderfully they just performed, their usual response is to give you reasons why it could have been done better, such as:

> I wasn't feeling quite up to it, but I did my best.
>
> It wasn't as smooth as I would have liked to have made it.
>
> I was really struggling to make it work.
>
> I did my best, and I guess I was just lucky today.

You're not hearing false modesty. These people actually believe that what they just did, which from our point of view was wonderful, could have actually been done better. And they will go home and study and practice so that the next time it will be better. The clear difference is that the also-rans think they have arrived some place, and the outstanding performers, the professionals, believe that they have not yet arrived.

Difference 4. Professionals Can Replicate Performance

By *replicate* I mean being able to perform the same tasks repeatedly without unnecessary deviation. Professionals can perform the same task, whether it be verbal or physical, over and over again to perfection. This is obviously the result of difference 3 above. They have practiced to perform that skill using the required tool, no matter what it is—a golf club, a scalpel, a basketball, or the voice and gestures of an actor and salesperson. Consistent performance is one of the true signs of a professional.

Difference 5. Professionals Don't Let Their Feelings Interfere with Their Performance

This is an important difference that never occurs to the non-professional. I was quite surprised the first time a doctor told me that in medical school he was encouraged to think of patients as medical subjects instead of personalities. The explanation, which later seemed obvious, was that when a doctor identifies emotionally with a patient, it can seriously affect the physician's ability to provide professional care. If a doctor felt emotionally about all sick patients, he or she would be too emotionally distraught to function. I have known nurses who could not make that professional separation in working with seriously ill cancer patients. They identified too much with the suffering of the patient and relatives and had to request a transfer out of that ward. I knew a psychologist who spent many years studying to work with brain-damaged children but became so emotionally involved with the patients that he became depressed and had to change his practice. I know a counselor who became so depressed when working with battered women that she changed her profession.

The professional's ability to separate feelings from performance relates to even more fundamental feelings. In our normal lives, if we are doing something that becomes boring or if it gets too hot or uncomfortable to do, we simply stop now and do it later, or not at all. We vary our performance according to how pressured we feel or uncomfortable or unhappy. For example, "I'm in a lousy mood today so I think I'll call in sick and not go to work." But when observing professionals perform, even in sports, being "too hot" or "too cold" or "too uncomfortable" is not an issue; if they have to do it, they do it in spite of how they feel about it. The professional's approach is epitomized in a response I got from a piano player who played nightly at a local restaurant. When I asked him how he felt about playing the same songs night after night as requested by the audience, his answer was, "I don't ask." I said, "What do you mean?" He said, "I don't ask myself how I feel about it because I might not like the answer. If I have to play these songs to make a living, I don't want to discover that I don't like it; otherwise, I'll have to live with that. So I just do what I have to do the best I possibly can and it works for me." He later admitted that he liked being a piano player but did not like every minute of playing the piano.

It seems that professionals have discovered something that the rest of us have not. They learned that the way they feel about doing something is separate from the importance of doing it or the actual doing of it. So if there is something that must be done well, they do it regardless of how they feel about it. You have undoubtedly heard that expression, "The show must go on." This means that actors must disregard their personal day-to-day problems, frustrations, and conflicts when they walk on stage. Professionals are able to do that.

Difference 6. Professionals Have a Plan

Surprisingly we found that the professionals and also-rans frequently exerted the same amount of energy in their performance. The critical difference was that the professionals' efforts were moving them closer to a specific goal. The professionals had specific goals and detailed plans on how to achieve them, but the also-rans were spinning their wheels. Few of the also-rans had specific goals, and most who did had no definite plans for how to achieve them. It appears that the professionals spend a lot of time thinking about where they want to be in life, whether for this Friday or for 10 years from now. They also spend a lot of time analyzing what they have to do to get from where they are now to where they want to be. The also-rans may work hard, but they make little progress in the right direction.

The overall conclusion from this analysis is that you don't become a professional because you have acquired degrees or because somebody gave you a specific title. It's the things you do today that make you a professional today. You are a professional when you act like one, and you stop being a professional when you stop acting like one.

To put this in perspective, you must realize that selling is not simply doing what comes naturally in life. It is more like a competitive athletic activity. In every selling situation there are specific things you must say and do to be successful. If you don't do them right or frequently enough or fast enough, you don't win. In any competitive game, whether it be tennis, golf, or football, the intensity of the activities is heightened because of the parameters that are set, such as boundaries, scorekeeping, and time limits for performance. Plus there is the presence of opposing players whose specific intention is to prevent you from being successful.

These things add an intensity to performance; they create those moments of truth, when the right thing must be done perfectly. Hardly any salesperson has a one-of-a-kind product that can be sold without competition. With almost any product you sell, there may be one to ten salespeople from different companies trying to sell their product which they say is better than yours. Because customers are buying products every day, there is also a time limit for you to be successful. You don't have all the time in the world to convince a particular customer that he or she should buy your product. If you wait too long, the customer will buy a similar, if not identical, product from someone else.

How to Use the Six Rules of Professionalism to Be a Winner

In selling, where the outcome of your performance is of critical importance to you and is achieved only by repeated excellent performance, professionalism is necessary for you to be successful. Converting the six differences between professionals and also-rans into six rules of professionalism gives you a personal guide to become a winner. You will be professional and outsell your competition and even your fellow salespeople if you follow these rules:

Rule 1. Do the Best
You Can Do

Whether you are trying to make a sale, trying to coordinate sales support activity internally in your own organization, or servicing an already-won customer, do what you have to do to perform perfectly for that situation. The secret is to avoid distractions and give your full attention to what you are trying to accomplish in each moment. Don't half-do what needs to be fully done, and don't put off till later what must be done now. Add to your personal rules of integrity, "If something is worth doing, then it's worth doing well."

Rule 2. Know Everything You
Need to Know

Study your product, your company, your competition's products, your customers, and the skills you use as a salesperson. You will receive a lot of useful information from your company; in fact, at times you will feel overwhelmed with the volume of it. But don't make the mistake of merely skimming it or burying it for study at a later date; study it now. And don't expect people to put all the needed information into your hands. Some of the information you will need about your customers and their marketplace you will have to gather yourself. Remember, if you only have general knowledge about what you're doing, you will be no better than everybody else. If you have detailed knowledge that others have not studied, you will be the expert. No sale was ever lost because a salesperson had too much knowledge.

Rule 3. Continue to Try
to Improve

One of life's biggest frustrations is failing. There is just nothing good about personal failure; it hurts; it costs time, money, reputation, and sometimes skin. But an even bigger frustration is not being able to answer the questions: "What went wrong?" "Why did I fail?" This is a bigger frustration because if you can't answer those questions, you are doomed to repeat your failure.

This sad fact is no more prevalent than in the selling profession. When you ask yourself, "Why didn't I get the sale?" and the answer is, "I don't know," you are lining up with the losers; you are going to repeat that failure.

Begin by analyzing your performance at the end of each sales call, at the end of each day, and at the end of each week to target the things you could have done better. Don't be satisfied with doing what comes naturally; strive to perform your selling job better than everybody else. When you conclude that you know everything you need to know or you're as good as you can ever be, you will stop trying to learn or improve and you will stop being a professional.

Rule 4. Be Able to Replicate Performance

Just as actors have to memorize their lines in order to portray a believable and impressive character on stage, you must memorize your lines to impress your customers. Write out the questions you want to ask and the answers you will have to give. Then practice, practice, practice them until you can deliver them flawlessly and with style. Practice your product demonstrations so that you can perform without hesitation or error.

Rule 5. Don't Let "How You Feel" Deny You Success

Work is work, and that's why they pay us to do it; if it were a lot of fun, we would have to pay to be permitted to do it. Remember the show business aspects of selling. As exciting as the selling profession is in general, repeating the same sales presentation six or seven or ten times a day can get to be boring. It's okay to be bored between sales calls, but it's not okay while you are on stage in front of the customer. Don't let your personal feelings dictate how hard you are going to work any day. Anybody can give up when the going gets tough or uncomfortable. When the going gets tough is when a professional breaks through what athletes call the pain barrier to go on to win.

Rule 6. Set Goals for Yourself and Make Plans to Achieve Them

One of your most limited resources is time—learn how to use it to its best effect. If you can only see your customers from 8 a.m. to 5 p.m., you must make maximum utilization of that time to achieve your sales goals. Get your priorities straight by first listing all the things you do each day and then rating them according to how much they contribute to your sales success and your career. When you know what is important, spend your time on the important things. In selling, as in many other things in life, it is the professional who is able to accomplish things in the time available—a feat that others say cannot be done.

These rules are summarized in Figure 1-1 on the following page. Rereading them frequently will keep you focused on what you need to do.

I WILL ACT LIKE A PROFESSIONAL

RULE NO. 1

I WILL DO THE BEST I CAN. I will give my full attention to what I am trying to accomplish in each moment and not half do what needs to be fully done or put off until later what must be done now.

RULE NO. 2

II WILL KNOW EVERYTHING I NEED TO KNOW. I will prepare myself to be knowledgeable about my company, my products, my customers, and my competition, and my marketplace.

RULE NO. 3

II WILL CONTINUOUSLY TRY TO IMPROVE. I will always seek knowledge and continue to study to raise my knowledge levels and I will use self-analysis to correct my weakness and improve my strength.

RULE NO. 4

II WILL BE ABLE TO REPLICATE PERFORMANCE. I will practice my performance until I am able to repeat it perfectly without deviation.

RULE NO. 5

II WILL NOT LET MY FEELINGS INHIBIT MY SUCCESS. I will perform at high levels as needed in spite of required repetitions and emotional distractions.

RULE NO. 6

II WILL SET PERFORMANCE GOALS AND MAKE PLANS TO ACHIEVE THEM. I will prioritize what I do to concentrate on those activities that contribute to goal achievement and modify my plans as necessary to adapt to changing conditions to meet my goals.

Figure 1-1. The six rules of professionalism.

2
Selling Is the Management of Buying

One of the most common but useless and dangerous salesperson descriptions of sales progress with a customer is "We are building a relationship." It is a useless comment because it does not specifically describe anything. And it is dangerous because once said, it implies the sale is progressing when in actuality nothing is happening except time is being wasted.

Salespeople who sell one-sales-call products, such as vacuum cleaners, some types of business equipment, office supplies, automobiles, and certain investments, have no doubts about sales progress after each sales call. If they leave with the customer's money, they won; if they didn't get the money, they lost. The nice part of selling one-call products is that it is easier to keep score on how you are doing. You get frequent feedback about what you are doing right and wrong, and you have frequent opportunities to change what you are doing to get better at it.

But selling a product requiring multiple sales calls is more difficult. It is not more difficult because the customer creates problems the salesperson can't handle; it is more difficult because there is no measurement of selling progress and the salesperson gets lost in the selling process. The best signal that this is happening is when a salesperson describes progress by saying, "I'm laying the groundwork," or "We are building relationships," or "I'm getting to know the customer." This response might sound okay if you didn't know anything about selling. But if you know something about selling, the answer tells you nothing. As a parallel example, picture yourself asking a golfer in the middle of his golf game how he is progressing and he answers, "I am getting to know the course." That response would not tell you anything specific about his progress. Since we normally count strokes per hole and know what par is for each hole on a course, we would expect a golfer to tell you his score as the number of strokes. Of course, you could interpret his answer to mean he has such poor ball control, he is wandering all over the course looking for his ball.

When teaching advanced sales skills to salespeople, I always ask how many sales calls are required for them to make the sale. They usually answer, "It depends," or "It could vary from 8 to 10 months," or "It takes as long as 3 years." Their answers invariably give numbers of months, not numbers of calls. When I push them to tell me how many *calls* are required, they say, "As many as it takes to get the sale."

The truth is they don't know how many calls it should take; they don't have a sales-call strategy. And that is why the multiple-call sale is difficult. The salesperson works hard making lots of visits to the customer, but the sale is not progressing in any measurable way. In other words, the salesperson is doing his selling thing, but the customer is not doing any buying.

Recently I was speaking at a national meeting to a group of salespeople whose product was a $25,000 chemical analysis machine sold to hospitals. When I asked them how many calls it took to sell their product to a hospital, they said it took 11 to 12 months to make a sale. When I asked them how many calls it should take to sell to a hospital, as a group they said it depends on a lot of things because all the customers were different. I pointed out to them that although all hospitals are different, they also share a lot of commonalities or else the salespeople would not be able to sell the same equipment to each hospital. Then I asked each to picture the profile of their average or most typical customer and tell me how many calls it would take to sell to that customer. By now we had a pretty good argument going. As a group, they were on their feet trying to convince me that I didn't know their business and that the selling process is too dynamic to be analyzed the way I was trying to do it.

When there was a lull in the yelling and screaming, a salesperson in the front row who had been quiet up to that point raised his hand and said, "Mr. Fournies, if I don't sell the product by the third call, I don't go back." A hush fell over the room because they all knew he was the highest-performing salesperson in the group. He went on to explain his approach as follows. He said, "On my first call I qualify the customer. I find out whether the customer needs my product and can afford it and who would make the buying decision if the hospital would buy it. If the answers are positive, I make an appointment for my next call. On my second call, I demonstrate the equipment to the buyer and all of the users and get them to make the buying decision. On the third call, I go back to pick up the purchase order."

When he finished talking, you could hear the proverbial pin drop. They were probably thinking what I was thinking: "If the most successful salesperson could do it in three sales calls (usually in less than 3 months), why did it take the other salespeople 11 months?" What were the rest of them doing and why? The answer is simple now that I know it, but it was not easy for me to discover. This is a common condition, but it is hidden to casual observation.

When I asked these salespeople taking 11 months to get the sale, "What is the objective of the last sales call you make with your customers?" they all said, "To get a signed order form and a purchase order for $25,000." When I asked them, "What is the objective of your first call?" the answers were:

To establish a relationship

To show them what we have to offer

To get to know them

To get my foot in the door

To demonstrate my equipment

To sell one unit

The big difference between the first and second answers seems puzzling. Why did they all answer the first question with the same specific answer but give differing and mostly nonspecific answers to the second question? The reason is that they know what they want the customer to do on the last call, but they don't know what they want the customer to do on the other calls. Also notice that some of the objectives described what the salesperson was going to do. This common problem with multiple-sales-call products stems from the confused definitions of selling.

After 20 years of selling things, teaching people how to sell things, and teaching managers how to manage people who sell things, the most functional definition of selling I've discovered is, "Selling is the management of buying." This means that salespeople do selling things so the customers will do buying things. It sounds simple, but the real dramatic impact of this definition is that since only customers do buying things, the objective of every sales call *must* describe the customer's action, not the salesperson's action. It is a small difference, but it is a major change in how selling activities are focused.

If you ask a vacuum cleaner salesperson just before her sales call what is the objective of this call, the quick answer will be "To get the cash or check for $229.95." Getting a customer to give her money is the objective of every sales call. If the salesperson leaves the customer's premises without the cash or check, that sales call was a failure. It is irrelevant that the salesperson may have impressed the customer with her in-depth product knowledge, quick wit, outgoing personality, charm, and dazzling display of her product. This vacuum cleaner salesperson knows that "no money" means "no sale." The salesperson has a definite recognizable *customer action objective* (CAO) for each sales call.

But with multiple-sales-call products, it's usually only the last call that has a specific measurable customer action objective because no such customer action objectives were established for the other calls. This problem is at its worst in the ethical pharmaceutical industry where the salesperson's job is to get doctors to prescribe the salesperson's product. When doctors get "sold," they don't purchase the product; they simply prescribe that product instead of what they formerly prescribed. But doctors only write prescriptions in front of patients, and the salesperson is never present when that happens. So the predominant sales-call objective in the industry is to get a doctor's "commitment," which means "The doctor will promise to prescribe my product."

This may sound reasonable under the circumstances, but if we evaluate that according to the basics of selling, that objective would be as useful as the vacuum cleaner salesperson having the sales-call objective of "The customer will promise to purchase my vacuum cleaner someday." A promise to buy may express an intent, but it is not a customer action that advances a sale. Promising to do something is vastly different from actually doing it.

Without measurable customer action as an objective, salespeople set objectives that describe what the salesperson will do, not what the customer will do, such as:

I will show.

I will demonstrate.

I will get to know.

If the customer is the only one doing the *buying things*, it must follow that the measurement of sales success must describe what the customer does, not what the salesperson does. If we compare the objective of the high-performing hospital salesperson with those of his bumbling peers, as well as the vacuum cleaner salesperson, it is easy to see that there is no difference in their ultimate sales goal. They all want the customer to sign the order form and give them a purchase order or cash. Purchase orders and cash are nice to deal with in sales; we have no trouble knowing whether it is in our hand or still in the customer's hand. If we analyze what the high-performing hospital salesperson does, we discover that he follows the principle that "Selling is the management of buying." He does this by establishing a specific measurable customer action objective for each sales call. Now here's the secret of his success: By establishing a specific, measurable customer action objective for each sales call, he creates the equivalent of an order form for every sales call as follows:

Call 1   The customer will describe to me the company's diagnostic needs, identify the decision maker for equipment purchases, indicate the current budget status, and give me an appointment to demonstrate my equipment.

Call 2   The customer's potential users will observe and use my equipment in a demonstration and verbally express their need and desire to own my equipment, and the decision maker will give me an expected quantity and date of purchase.

Call 3   The customer will sign my order form and give me a purchase order for one or more units of our equipment.

The high-performing salesperson knew exactly what he wanted the customer to do on *every* sales call, just as all the other salespeople knew what they wanted the customer to do on the *last* sales call. He didn't write it down each time, although he could have. By setting a measurable objective for each call describing what the customer would do on that call (CAO) to denote success of that sales call, he established the basis for the two most important aspects of selling success:

1. Before that sales call he could plan the specific selling things he needed to do to manage the customer on that call to achieve the call objective.

2. He could gauge his progress during and after the call to know whether or not he was winning or losing.

If we look again at what the high-performing salesperson did, it is obvious that he created a three-call selling strategy to manage the progression of the sale. He recognized that he had to accomplish the call objective of call 1 before he could make call 2; and he had to accomplish the objective of call 2 before he could move to call 3. He had an overall sales goal or sales objective which is what he wanted the customer to do eventually as a result of all the sales calls. And he had individual measurable sales-call objectives for each separate sales call. He knew where he was going, what he had to do to get there, and whether or not he was winning or losing along the way. His bumbling peers had an overall sales goal but no strategy or plan on how to achieve it. They were taking 11 months to make or lose the sale because of the following:

Their emphasis was on what they were doing (selling things), not on what they wanted the customer to do (buying things).

They tried to achieve the third-call objective without achieving objectives for call 1 or 2.

They sometimes made call 2 before they accomplished the objective of call 1.

They required several calls to achieve the objective of one sales call.

Their call activities were not goal-directed. Therefore, they had no accumulative influence on the customer; the sale did not progress over time.

This brings us to another principle I learned the hard way: If you don't know before a sales call what you want a customer to do on that call, don't make that call, because you will waste your time.

How to Create a Sales Strategy

The reason multiple sales calls are needed to sell some products is because there are too many things (selling things and buying things) to be done on one call. The exception would be calling on a customer the second time because you failed to get the sale the first time.

In multiple-call selling, each sales call should have an accumulated effect in moving (managing) the customer closer to the ultimate buying decision (action). If this were not so, a multiple-call strategy would not be needed; all products would be sold on a one-call sale. Of course, the selling job would be a lot easier and a lot less expensive if all products were a one-call sale. Unfortunately, most outside sale products require multiple sales calls.

After getting you this far, your obvious question probably is, "How many sales calls should I make on any customer?" The sure answer is, "Only as many as you need." Determining the right number of calls is a by-product of creating your sales strategy. It would be nice if the company you worked for had already created the optimum sales strategy, but unfortunately the majority of companies have not done so—and it never ceases to amaze me that they have not. An even sadder fact is that in those companies that have developed a detailed sales strategy, some salespeople ignore it and waste their time trying to reinvent the wheel.

If you are creating your own sales strategy, a good approach is to do it backward; start with the objective of the last call and work backward. Using this backward approach invariably produces the shortest selling strategy, getting the sale with the least number of sales calls. If you were one of those hospital salespeople and I was helping you create a selling strategy, our discussion would probably go like this:

ME: You and I are going to work out a selling strategy for selling your equipment to hospitals. When we are finished, you will have a basic strategy that you can apply to your typical customer. You will always have a few customers who for some reason will not be typical, but you will still be able to modify your strategy to create a selling plan to fit that customer. The objective is not to force the customer into a fixed mold but to create an approach that will work with most of your customers. To begin with, what is the overall sales goal with the typical hospital?

YOU: To sell them one or more of our machines.

ME: How would we recognize that if we achieved it?

YOU: What do you mean?

ME: What will the customer do or say so we will say, "Aha, we got the sale"?

YOU: The customer will sign our order form and give us a purchase order number.

ME: Why doesn't he do that now?

YOU: He may not know that our equipment is available and that we want him to buy it.

ME: Is there any reason why we couldn't just call him on the phone or go over there and ask for the purchase order?

YOU: He wouldn't do that.

ME: Why?

YOU: He doesn't know anything about our equipment and why he should buy it.

ME: Okay, why don't we send some literature to him or drop it off and then ask him to give us a purchase order?

YOU: He wouldn't do that.

ME: Why not? Our literature will describe our equipment.

YOU: Well, he might not read the literature. And if he did, he might have questions and he might not be convinced that he should spend $25,000 on new equipment.

ME: What would we have to do to make sure he knows about our equipment and to convince him that he needs it?

YOU: We would have to demonstrate our equipment to him, showing him how the speed and accuracy would save him operating costs.

ME: Is there any reason why we couldn't go over there and do a demonstration now and get the purchase order?

YOU: Well, he would probably not buy it unless his staff thought it was a good idea.

ME: What do we have to do to get the staff to agree it is a good idea to buy our equipment?

YOU: We have to demonstrate to them also.

ME: Is there any reason why we can't go over there and do that now?

YOU: Yes. You just don't walk into a laboratory and ask people to stop what they are doing for an hour to watch our demonstration. Also, the demonstration is only effective if it is related to their real work, their current process, current number of staff, work load, etc. Besides, they may not be able to afford to buy our equipment even if they wanted it, and we would be wasting our time.

ME: What do we have to do?

YOU: We have to talk to the lab people and find out what they are doing, what their work load is, their staffing, etc., and identify who actually makes the buying decision and whether they have a budget to buy.

ME: Is there any reason why we can't go over their now and do that?

YOU: No.

Great. What we have just done is to create a selling strategy in reverse. By doing it backward you invariably end up with the minimum number of sales calls in your strategy. By asking the question "Why can't we go over there and do that now?" you sidestep the two traps of:

1. Making sales calls you don't need to make.
2. Expecting to get the sale without making enough sales calls.

When asking groups of salespeople selling multiple-call products what are the objectives of their first sales call, sometimes they answer, "To get the sale." When I ask them how many ever got the sale on the first call, the usual response is "No one." But they often argue that if you could get the sale on the first call, you should take it. In general that is true. But if a multiple-call strategy is needed to sell your product, it means that certain things must be accomplished on a number of previous calls so you will get the sale on the last call. If you try to get the sale on the first call, you will fail because the customer is not yet ready to buy. However, if you walk in to see a customer on the first call and she says, "I will buy it," take the order. Don't worry about being inconsistent with the first-call objective. Don't pass up an opportunity for the customer to buy. But also don't confuse rare opportunities (surprises) with selling strategy.

How to Set Customer Action Objectives

That brings us to the next step, which is reducing our overall selling strategy to a sales-call strategy. Since the above backward analysis tells us generally what has to be done to get the sale, we now need to establish the optimum number of sales calls required and a CAO for each sales call. A CAO is composed of the following:

1. It must be an observable action by the customer.
2. The action must occur on this sales call.
3. The action must advance the sale (manage the customer closer to buying).

Within these guidelines, and using the above backward analysis, let's resume our previous discussion.

ME: What would you say is the objective of the first sales call?

YOU: I want to meet some of the laboratory people and learn something about the operating budget and who does the buying.

ME: Wait a minute. You are describing what you are going to do. That is not a CAO. What will the customer do on the first call so you know whether or not you are winning or losing?

YOU: Well, laboratory technicians will tell me their names, tell me the kinds of analysis they are doing, describe their volume of work, name the person who makes the buying decisions, and generally indicate whether they are on a tight or loose budget for capital expenditures.

ME: That's good. You met all the requirements of a CAO. If the customer does all that on the first call, you will achieve your first sales-call objective. Another way of looking at it is that what you described as a CAO is really the product you are selling for that call. If you get the customer to do that on that call, you actually got the sale for that call. Okay, now what?

YOU: Using the information the customer gave me, I decide whether or not to go back with a product demonstration. If the hospital doesn't have the budget or if the volume of work is too low to benefit from my equipment, I will not go back. If the customer has potential, I will make an appointment.

ME: When do you decide that?

YOU: After the call.

ME: Is it easy for you to decide that while you're on the first call?

YOU: Yes, but why rush?

ME: The question is not, "Why rush?" the question is, "Why waste time?" If you are in front of the customer and you know you want to come back to demonstrate your product, you should get an appointment then and there.

YOU: I see. So I should add to my CAO for the first call, "If the customer meets my potential requirements, he or she will give me an appointment to demonstrate my product."

ME: Great. But on your second call will you demonstrate it to the staff first and then to the decision maker, or to both on the same call?

YOU: I could include both in the one demonstration.

ME: Right. So what you must add to the customer action objective for the first call is, "if the customer meets my potential requirements, he or she will give me an appointment to demonstrate my equipment to the buyer and the staff simultaneously." Okay so far. What is the CAO of the second call?

YOU: To demonstrate my equipment.

ME: No, that is what you will be doing. That is a selling thing. What do you want the customer to do because you demonstrated your equipment?

YOU: Ah,...the customer will state that with my equipment he or she can run more analyses in a shorter time with greater accuracy, eliminate erroneous reports to doctors and avoid legal battles with patients, and expand services to provide things the hospital doesn't have time for now. The people I'm working with will state that they want my equipment, pick a location for it, sign the order blank, and give me a date when I can come back to pick up the purchase order.

ME: I think you've got it. What next?

YOU: Make the next call. The CAO is the customer will give me an authorized purchase order for one or more of my machines.

ME: So now you have a three-call sales strategy with a CAO for each call.

Please understand that this three-call strategy is only an example. The product you sell may be a one-call or a ten-call product. Also, the sales-call strategy you develop is only appropriate for your typical or most common type of customer. It is a guide, not a straitjacket. You will shorten your strategy when opportunities arise and lengthen it when things are not progressing as you planned. You will also use the same kind of analysis to plan special selling strategies for those customers who, for whatever reason, differ widely from the norm. Once you start selling according to a plan, you'll be surprised how many of your customers fit the norm.

In applying this concept of CAO in ethical pharmaceutical sales, we have gotten salespeople to stop relying on doctors' promises and to set more measurable actions that could be considered as getting the sale, such as:

The doctor will write a patient's name on a product starter dose (sample).

The doctor will put a note in the patient's folder as a reminder to prescribe our product the next time the patient comes in.

The doctor will give me permission to change his standing orders to include our product.

The doctor will write a prescription for my product for a hypothetical patient.

It is important for your success to create a selling strategy so you don't make ten calls to sell a three-call product or try to sell a ten-call product in three calls. The next step is to make a plan of what selling things you will have to do on each call in order to get the customer to do the buying things of your CAO. The remainder of this book will help you do that.

Stop Confusing Service Calls with Sales Calls

As a salesperson, you will probably be making service calls as well as sales calls on your customers. Amazing as it may seem, the majority of salespeople do not know the difference between them; therefore, they think they are working hard selling when they are in fact only servicing. If you confuse the two, you will work hard but not understand why you are not getting as many sales as you think you should get. Some marketing departments, as well as salespeople, confuse themselves with the motto "Good service leads to good sales," and so they are not concerned about the difference between the two.

It is undeniable that poor customer service to existing customers will help you lose repeat business, and good customer service will help you generate repeat business. And both good and bad customer service contribute to a reputation that can influence future sales. But the fact is that if you have the best service in the world but you don't sell effectively, you will have fewer customers to service. The way for you to tell the difference between a sales call and a service call becomes clear when you set the CAO for the call. The objective of all sales calls describes what the customer will do on the call, but the objective of all service calls describes what you, the salesperson, will do on that call. Here are some examples of service-call objectives:

I will correct the customer's misunderstanding about our credit agreement.

I will train the customer's employees on how to operate our equipment.

I will give the customer the specifications for the new installation.

I will inventory and prepare the return of outdated products.

I will show the customer how to plan her parts inventory.

I will explain the mix-up in the shipping dates.

I will show the customer how to cancel his old lease agreement.

I will set up a product display.

These are quite different from the following CAOs:

The buyer will introduce me to the director of research.

The customer will give me a printout of his insurance claims for the past 24 months.

The customer will give me a date for installing our equipment as a test on 10 percent of her terminals.

The customer will give me three credit references.

The customer will allocate the space for the installation of display racks.

The customer will give me $400 to participate in our co-op advertising program.

The customer will give me permission to begin an analysis of his inventory usage on the 15th of next month.

Comparing these examples clearly reveals that on service calls *you* are doing things for the customer and on sales calls you expect the customer to do things for you. Both service calls and sales calls advance the sale, but service calls occur generally after you make the sale and sales calls occur before you make the sale.

One of the most dramatic examples of this confusion between selling and servicing is found in newspaper space sales. Most newspaper space salespeople not only sell space to customers but also write the advertising copy. I pointed out to one newspaper client that their salespeople were spending 80 percent of their time writing copy, running back and forth to customers finalizing copy, and trying to collect from no-pay customers. Sales were not growing because the salespeople were not spending enough time doing actual selling things; they were spending only 20 percent of their time selling. Management was also unhappy because of the high turnover in salespeople; many left within 12 months. I pointed out that people who like to sell generally don't like to write copy, and people who like to write copy generally don't like to sell. The newspaper would be a lot more successful if it hired a few people to write all the copy and permitted their salespeople to devote 100 percent of their time to selling. Sales would increase using a smaller sales force, and the customers would probably get better advertising copy.

Your success as a salesperson will depend on a lot of things, and only one of them is knowing the difference between selling and servicing. One of the secrets to outselling everyone else is to make more sales calls per day than everyone else. Another secret is to call on customers with the highest potential for buying your product (to be covered in a future chapter). Still another secret is to not make more sales calls on any customer than necessary to get the sale.

In a later chapter you will learn more about the importance of using time management to maximize your success and earnings. But the critical understanding that underlies all your selling efforts is that selling is not hanging around being nice to people in some random fashion. If you don't establish a sales strategy and CAO for each of your sales calls, you will be wasting your time:

1. Trying to do on one call what can only be done on multiple calls

2. Making more calls than necessary to get the same sale

You will lose sales because there will be no system to your selling activities and you will not be managing the buying process. To keep yourself focused, memorize this definition of selling:

SELLING IS THE MANAGEMENT OF BUYING; I DO SPECIFIC AND NECESSARY SELLING THINGS TO GET THE BUYER TO DO SPECIFIC AND NECESSARY BUYING THINGS.

3

The Time
of Your Life

If you're over 16 years old, you've probably been told that the most important resource in your life is time. On birthdays it's usual for some older relative to say, "Use your time wisely, young person. You don't live forever." Or possibly you have heard, "Never put off until tomorrow what you can do today," or "The early bird catches the worm," or "Time waits for no one," or "It is what you do with time, not time itself, that is worth money." The one I like is "Time is a fixed income, and as with any income, the real problem facing most of us is how to live successfully within our daily allotment."[1]

But in spite of all this sage advice, most people under 50 don't pay a lot of attention to time; they take it for granted the same way they accept breathing as a natural course of events. When we are young, this advice sounds like a bunch of non-sense because there are so many more important things to worry about each day—and besides, we're going to live forever.

The underlying message about time, of course, is that the clock is ticking all the time, whether you're sleeping or awake, and once a minute is past, it is gone forever; it is never coming back. It is not at all like money. You can save money, or you can decide to spend it or change your mind about spending it, and you can usually earn more if you need it. But time is a mindless resource that just keeps rolling along. It doesn't stop when you

[1]Margaret B. Johnstone, *Lifetime Speakers Encyclopedia,* Prentice Hall, 1962.

say, "Hey, wait a minute, wait a minute. I wasn't ready. Give me another chance."

One reality of life is that there never seems to be enough time to do all the things you want to do, whether it be work or play. But this "Time waits for no one" problem is even more critical in selling because you can't choose to call on customers any time you want to. In most selling situations, customers are not available 24 hours a day, 7 days a week. Some customers will only talk to salespeople one day of each week or month. Some doctors, for example, will give only one appointment per year to a salesperson.

11 Typical Time Wasters

When sales managers discuss the reasons why salespeople fail, one of the common reasons mentioned is poor utilization of time. Some of the typical time wasters mentioned are:

1. Calling on customers who don't need or who can't afford your product
2. Making selling presentations to people who don't make or influence the buying decision
3. Doing things in person that could be done effectively by phone, by mail, or by fax
4. Spending excessive time traveling between customers
5. Disrupting planned daily sales-call schedules for unimportant reasons
6. Calling on customers more frequently than necessary to get the same amount of sales
7. Not calling on customers frequently enough
8. Making service calls during high-selling periods by day, week, month, or season
9. Working on paperwork during high-selling periods
10. Calling on customers at the wrong time (day, week, month)
11. Not working a full day

Except for the last item, salespeople who do these things are not goofing off. They're working hard. They're just not working on things that will give them the best sales return for the time invested. One reason for this pervasive problem in selling is that salespeople have not connected with the idea that their selling time is an investment and their personal sales are the return from that investment.

When conducting sales seminars for experienced salespeople, one of my favorite exercises is to ask them how much time they spend selling each week. Their usual response varies from 40 to 50 hours per week. I then explain that I didn't ask them how many hours they work each week; I asked them how much time they spend in actually selling each week. When they ask me what I mean, I explain that selling only occurs when you are within hearing distance or smelling distance of the customer. You are not selling while you are driving your car between customers; you are not selling while you are sitting in waiting rooms; and you are not selling while you are checking customers' inventory levels. You are only selling when either you are face to face with the customers or you are speaking to them by phone.

When I then ask them to calculate how many minutes they spend in their 40- to 50-hour week actually within hearing distance or smelling distance of the customer, the number changes dramatically. For example, salespeople who make seven sales calls per day averaging 15 minutes per sales call will spend only 8.75 hours actually selling in a 5-day workweek. The rest of their time, which is not selling time, is spent traveling, preparing to sell, and perhaps servicing customers. Some of these things may be supportive of the selling process, but they cannot be included in actual selling time.

Notice I am not even talking about the effectiveness of the selling time. I'm merely talking about the amount of selling time. If you have two salespeople of equal selling ability but one spends 11 hours each week in actual selling time and the other spends only 7 hours per week, all else being equal, the first salesperson will get more sales.

Some salespeople have difficulty understanding this fact that selling only takes place when they are within hearing distance or smelling distance of the customer—they say that everything they do is related to selling. They are missing the point. We can make the same comparison in a sport, such as golf. You certainly need golf clubs to play the game, and you either carry your bag or use a caddy or rent a golf cart. But no matter how much money you pay for your golf clubs and golf clothes, and no matter how much time you spend polishing your clubs, your shoes, and your Mercedes golf cart and practicing your stroke, you are only playing golf when you swing your golf club at the ball on the course. We can even say that looking for your lost ball in the rough, or fishing for it in the water, is not playing golf. It is getting ready to play golf—if you can find your ball.

So one secret to sales success is understanding the cost-benefit relationship of your selling activities. Your major investment (cost) in your success is your selling time; your major return (benefit) on that investment is your sales dollars and ultimately your compensation (commission and bonus). Return on investment to you is the amount of sales you get for the amount of time and effort you expend in selling activities.

One interesting measure of your sales effectiveness is how much sales return you get per selling minute. You can calculate that by dividing your total sales dollars for any period by the number of minutes you spent in selling to customers for that period (in person or by phone). For example, if you produced $2,500,000 in sales from your territory last year and you spent an average of 2 hours per day actually talking to customers, you could calculate how much sales you generated per selling minute as follows:

Annual sales dollars you generate	$2,500,000
Minutes per day *with* customers	120 minutes
Days worked per year	250 days
Minutes per year with customer	30,000 minutes

$$\frac{\$2,500,000}{30,000} = \$83.33 \text{ sales dollars per minute}$$

In this example your sales return on a selling minute of your time is $83.33.

If you make the same calculation based on your earned bonus or commission, you would have even a more dramatic understanding of the value of your selling time. For example, if you are paid a salary but you also earned $10,000 in bonus last year, spending the same 2 hours per day actually selling to customers earned you $0.33 bonus per selling minute. It doesn't sound like much, but you could correctly assume that if you increased your selling time in front of customers by 30 minutes per day, your bonus could increase by almost $2475 per year. Your increased selling time would permit you to be more effective with current customers or more likely would increase the number of customers you would see per year.

How to Take Control of Your Time

Of course, the objective in selling is always to get the maximum sales dollar return for every sales minute invested, but you must first achieve maximum selling time in your workweek.

If you're not sure that you need to worry about using your time more effectively, you can ask yourself the following questions:

1. Is my actual selling time more than that of my peers? (You may not be able to answer this question if your peers are not calculating their selling time.)
2. Is my income as much as I'd like it to be?
3. Are there things I want to do that I can't get done?

Negative answers to these questions would indicate that better time management would help you achieve more in life. One result of poor time management is being rushed in everything you do. You never seem to have any time to spare; you rush from place to place, arriving late occasionally and not doing a lot things, such as planning, call analysis, and follow-up with customers.

Your first step to control your time is to find out how you are presently using it. Begin by listing all your daily activities, such as driving, phoning to make appointments, writing activity reports, sitting in waiting rooms, checking customer's inventory, preparing proposals, filling out expense reports, talking to customer's staff, etc. Don't try to limit the number of categories. For example, "doing paperwork" may be too broad because it refers to preparing proposals as well as expense reports. The longer the list is, the more effective it will be in breaking down your activities into specific categories you can deal with.

Next, enter approximately how much time you spend each day on each of these activities. You may not be able to do this off the top of your head—you may have to spend a few days keeping track of how you spend your time.

As a third step, classify each item as (1) having direct influence on getting a sale, (2) having indirect influence on getting a sale, or (3) having no effect on getting a sale. For example, "talking to customers about new products" would have direct influence. "Talking to customers about problems with billing" would be category 2. "Sitting in waiting rooms" would be category 3, having no impact on sales. Don't use more than three categories or a numbering system such as 1–5 or 1–10 because the classification will be meaningless to you.

After you finish, look at each item in category 3 and ask yourself, "Why am I doing this at all?" If the answer is, "I must do it or I will get fired," the second question is, "Can I do it at some time other than during peak selling periods?" If you're really serious about releasing more selling time during the workweek, you will find ways of eliminating things that do not have to be done at all or reschedule them for low-selling periods of the day or week.

You will also find ways of doing things faster; for example, get out a map and plot the actual route you followed in visiting customers on a particular day and ask yourself if you could have saved time by picking a different route. You may discover that you don't have a plan at all and you are driving excessive miles to see the same number of customers. You may be driving past customers you could have visited if you changed your schedule. You may find ways of avoiding traffic delays by rescheduling appointments around morning and evening commuter delays.

Also identify the things that interrupt your plans. For example, how do you respond when customers call you with a problem? Do you disrupt today's schedule to visit them? You might accomplish the same result by handling the problem by phone or scheduling the solution for another time without disrupting today's schedule.

9 Rules That Save Travel Time

If you want to economize your travel time, here are nine basic rules to follow:

1. Use maps to plot your customer locations, and plan your routing in the order you need to see your customers.
2. Divide your territory into quadrants or zones containing enough customers for you to see in each zone each day, and schedule your time to remain in that zone to save travel time.
3. Include more customers in your daily plan than you need so cancellations don't hurt your call rate for the day. If you want to see seven customers, plan to see ten.
4. Don't do in person what you can do by phone or fax.
5. When possible, do not disrupt today's schedule to respond to a customer request unless it is an emergency.
6. Before disrupting today's schedule to respond to a customer request, always verify by phone that it is necessary to disrupt today's schedule to respond.
7. Schedule customers to minimize travel time.
8. Arrange call frequency of customers to eliminate traveling past customers who could be called on.
9. Arrange your daily or weekly schedule to group office things together and field things together to eliminate unnecessary travel between the office and the field.

You may also find that your schedule frequently gets disrupted because you have to wait 30 minutes or more to see a customer. One solution is to make appointments. With those customers who make you wait inordinate amounts of time even when you have an appointment, don't wait. Or if a customer makes you wait more than 15 minutes, schedule another appointment and go on to complete your schedule for that day.

When your analysis is finished, one of the most likely conclusions you will come to is that there are certain things you are now doing during the day that you will have to start doing in the evening or on weekends because they are interfering with your daily selling time.

You have to have a plan of what you want to do with your time. You can't begin your workday by saying, "Gee, I wonder which customer I will call on today." You have to plan your schedule one, two, or three weeks in advance: Whom you are going to call on? In what order and in what frequency? And for what purpose? Don't call on customers merely because you are in the area. Call on them because you need to manage the buying to advance the sale.

Don't plan your maximum number of sales calls per day according to how many your company requires. Set that number according to how many you need to make to get maximum sales. If the company requires seven calls a day and you can do nine, why in the world are you doing seven if you want to be an outstanding sales achiever? I knew one salesperson who made more sales calls than anybody else simply because he walked faster than everybody else.

How to Stop
Wasting Time

One subtle aspect of poor time management is the problem of spending time in front of customers who have little or no potential as buyers. This can vary the full spectrum from customers who are not decision makers to customers who wouldn't use your product even if you gave it to them because they don't need it.

In reality, everybody in the world is a customer for some product. The big question is whether every customer has the potential for buying your product or buying as much of your product as you need to sell. Spending a lot of hours making very effective sales presentations to customers who have little or no potential for buying your product is a bad investment of selling time. To avoid doing that you have to identify customer potential by identifying who are the most likely buyers of your product. Some questions that will help you to do that are as follows:

1. What is the profile of the typical buyer of my product?
2. Who fits that profile whether or not they are using products like ours now?
3. Who in that organization is the person who most likely makes the buying decision?
4. What is the best time to call on that person (hour of the day, week, or month)?
5. How many times do I have to call on that person in order to make the sale?
6. What is the most effective frequency for making those calls?

It is up to you to collect enough information to classify or qualify each contact as a high- or low-potential customer. The first step is to create one profile of the people most likely to buy your products and another profile of the people least likely to buy your products. If your company didn't originate its business yesterday, this will be less difficult because statistics about current and past customers will be available. Your company may have already created a profile of the high- and low-potential customers—use it. If it hasn't created one, create your own. Below is a beginning list of categories to include in your profile.

1. *Size of the Business.* Identify the organization size of customers who typically buy your product. Size could relate to number of employees, annual sales, number of offices, etc. If you find that companies with gross annual sales less than $1 million never or rarely buy your products, you have identified a low-potential factor. If you find that companies with 500 or more employees usually buy your product, you have found a high-potential factor. There are a lot of customer

aspects other than annual sales which may be more relevant to your product, such as the number of states in which the customer has branch offices, the growth rate, the number of vehicles in the customer's fleet, the number of computers used, the amount of scrap or effluent produced, etc.

2. *Experience in Using Similar Products.* If your product requires a lot of customer preparation to use it, the client who is already using a similar product would have a high potential. It would be easier (quicker) for that customer to switch to your product than for a customer who has never used that kind of product. The customer who has never used your kind of product would have to make a more encompassing business decision requiring the expenses of preparation, training, etc., before beginning to use your product. This may be considered a low potential in that it would take more time to make the sale. However, if the sales benefit from converting this type of customer is quite profitable for your company, it could be a high-potential factor in spite of the time factor.

3. *Competitive Product Currently Used.* Your product will have features and benefits and price advantages over some competitive products and not over others. Customers currently using competitive products superior to yours would be low potential. Customers using competitive products you can easily blitz have higher potential.

The categories you include in your profile can be as many and as varied as there are companies selling products. Depending on your product, you might include:

All companies going into Chapter 11

All companies coming out of Chapter 11

All companies going into a merger

All families having their first child

All households with a second mortgage

All companies owning an automobile fleet

All companies owning a company airplane

All companies selling outside the United States

All companies using rail transport

All individuals with disposable income of $10,000 or more per year

All restaurants with a delivery or takeout service.

The important point in creating your profile is not to pick a category, but to find it. Analyze what your current high-sales customers have in common. That tells you what categories should be in the profile. But keep an open mind, or creative opportunities will not occur to you, such as selling fax machines to restaurants for takeout orders. One seller of financial planning services described doctors as the popular target of salespeople, but doctors, he said, are overprospected and average only $4000 in savings annually. Since 80 percent of U.S. millionaires own small businesses, better prospects would be truck-stop owners, turkey farmers, and widows of hog farmers.

Your objective is to perform those activities that have the most direct relationship to getting the most sales from customers with the highest potential at the most profit.

PART 2

How to See the World through Your Customers' Eyes

4

They Don't Do Dumb Things on Purpose

Whenever salespeople get together, they inevitably swap stories about the ecstasies of sales success and the agonies of defeat. You can hear the blow-by-blow description of the dazzling footwork of the valiant nimble-minded self-sacrificing narrator who got the sale in spite of the plodding unresponsiveness of his own company and the intransigent customer. You can hear euphoric descriptions of the big windfall sale that took little or no effort, as well as the sorrowful disappearance of the down payment on the ski-country condo because the customer went into Chapter 11. But you will also hear about those "dumb customers":

I gave him the lowest price in the industry, and he still would not buy.

He made the specifications so tough, no one could deliver the product he wanted.

No matter what I told her about the quantity discounts, she wouldn't give me a big order.

I told her that the competition would not deliver what they promised, but she gave them the order anyhow.

I showed him on paper that what he is using now will cause

him higher maintenance costs two to three years in the future, but the dummy would not switch.

These "dumb customer" stories, which always blame the customer for the lost sale, are the saddest stories, because the salesperson who failed has not learned from his failure. When the salesperson says, "I can't understand why that customer did that dumb thing," he is describing the real cause of the lost sale; he does not understand the total selling situation.

To understand customers and the seemingly dumb things they do, you need to have a broader understanding of people in general. You don't have to be a psychologist, but it would help to know some basic things psychologists know. For example, psychologists tell us that "everything a person does seems like a good idea to that person at that time." In other words, people don't do dumb things on purpose. The things a person does which seem dumb to us only appear that way because we are looking at the world or that situation from our point of view. We're not looking at it from the other person's point of view. If we understood how a person viewed and interpreted a particular situation, we would have understood why the person acted a certain way in that situation. This does not mean that you would have done the same thing or even agree with it. But you would understand why the person did it.

The vast knowledge we have about human motivation supports the simple conclusion that people take action in the world to acquire desirable things (to make life brighter) or to avoid undesirable things (also to make life brighter). Desirable things could be tangible things we can touch and measure, such as money, physical comfort, convenience, improved physical powers or muscle size, ice cream, the ability to do something with less effort, a savings in time as a result of doing something faster, etc. Desirable things can also be intangible things, which are more symbolic and difficult to measure, such as happiness, improved social or professional status, increased feelings of security, an expression of love or admiration, improved religious state, etc.

The avoidance of unpleasant things, which include solving a current problem or preventing a future one, could also be tangible or intangible. Tangibles could be decreasing pain, making broken things work, eliminating loss and waste, decreasing complaints, avoiding legal problems, etc. The intangibles could be protecting against loss of love, image, or reputation; avoiding social rejection; or not making your boss angry, etc. As a generalization we could say that people are moved to acquire things (tangible and intangible), and once those things are acquired, people are not moved unless they can lose those things. This is a good basis for understanding people's buying motives—the reason they spend their money to buy things.

Your understanding of each customer's buying motives is crucial to your success as a salesperson because you need the customer's cooperation to get his money. If you could get the customer's money without his cooperation, it would be called robbery, and robbery rarely results in repeat business or career longevity. Whenever you don't understand the customer's buying motives, you will not understand the total selling situation and you will blame the customer for your failures.

One simple truth about selling is that you will only get maximum cooperation from your customers if the things you want them to do make sense to them. This means that your analysis of all selling situations must be from the customer's (or prospect's) point of view.

5
They Don't Tell Us What They Mean

One of the strange things about people (and this includes customers) is that they frequently don't say what they mean or mean what they say. If you review your own experience with acquaintances and friends, you will discover examples similar to the following:

People say they will never do something but eventually do it.

People say they will stop doing something but continue to do it.

People profess strong beliefs about a certain subject but act in conflict with their professed beliefs.

People say they cherish certain things, but in action they abuse those very same things they cherish.

The easy explanation for this conflict between what people say and what they do is that people lie a lot. But that would explain away only a small percentage. You could also say that people don't really know what they mean or that they change their minds frequently. But that would explain away only another small percentage. The major reason people don't say what they mean is that people are sloppy communicators; they don't say what they mean because they don't know how to accurately say it. Most people talk in shorthand and metaphors and use nonverbal body motions and facial expressions which communicate ambiguously. People say, "I could kill for a cold beer right now," or "I am dying to go to Hawaii for a week's vacation," but actual death is not what they are talking about. Here are two friends talking:

FRIEND: Hi Frank, how is it going?

FRANK: It's a bummer.

FRIEND: Having a bad day?

FRANK: Hey, it's Monday, you know.

FRIEND: Ho, ho, big weekend, eh?

FRANK: No, I just fell apart today, and the boss is on my case.

FRIEND: What's eating him?

FRANK: He's into his boss thing, you know.

FRIEND: Oh, wow, I have to run. Hang in there. Catch you later.

As a social contact, this conversation seems normal. But if you were required to do something about Frank's problem, it would be useless. There is certainly some general information being exchanged, but there are no specifics. You would have to question Frank to find out specifically what he means by:

"bummer"

"it's Monday"

"I just fell apart"

"on my case"

"boss thing"

As a salesperson, you face the same communication problem when dealing with your customers; they also use verbal shorthand and ambiguous terms. But understanding what they say to you is crucial to understanding their point of view. When a customer says, "it is too expensive," does he mean:

I can't afford to buy it.

OR

I can buy the same thing for less money from someone else.

OR

It is not well made for the price.

OR

The benefits I expect from owning it are not worth the price of buying it.

OR

I will buy it, but let's see if I can get a lower price.

When the customer says, "We will think about it," does he mean:

I don't understand what you told me.

OR

I'm not sure I should buy it.

OR

I need someone else's approval.

OR

This is a good way to get this salesperson out of my office.

Some people will purchase what they want to own regardless of price. Some people will purchase things only because the price is high. There are people who will purchase what they don't need if the price is right. There are people who will not purchase what they want because the price is too high. There are people who will not purchase what they need (like medicine) because the price is too high. There are people who want what they don't need and who don't want what they do need. And there are people who want what is bad for them. There is a big difference between "want" and "need," with nuances of each. For example, the following comments don't mean the same thing.

It is well made.

I would like to own it.

I need it.

I will buy it.

From a salesperson's point of view, these statements are positive; the customer is expressing an interest in the product. But each statement taken alone could be misleading. Appreciating the quality of a product does not mean the customer would like to own it. Wanting to own a product does not mean the customer is willing to pay for that privilege. Needing something does not mean the customer wants to own it or is willing to pay for it. Agreeing to buy a product communicates an intent to exchange the customer's money for the product but says nothing about the customer's wants, needs, or ability to pay for the purchase.

Most books and seminars about selling mention the use of questioning techniques to understand the customer's buying situation, but they don't stress how critical those techniques are for selling success. Consequently, the majority of salespeople across all product lines ask questions badly for the following reasons:

They don't ask enough (or any) questions.

They ask questions but don't wait for the customer to answer.

They interrupt when the customer is talking.

They accept nonspecific answers.

They ask difficult-to-answer questions too soon, and so the customer resists answering.

They don't know what customer information they need to know.

They disregard the customer's answers.

If you don't understand what the customer is talking about, you will not understand the customer's point of view. Therefore, your responses will not be appropriate to that customer and you will lose sales unnecessarily.

How to Understand
the Customer's
Point of View

1. The only way for you to understand the customer's point of view is to have the customer describe it to you. Since most customers don't volunteer to do that and those who do give incomplete or ambiguous descriptions, the burden of collecting complete information is yours. Asking good questions will get more sales for you.

2. You don't have to become a mind reader or psychologist to understand the customer's point of view. You only have to collect the relevant information. The most effective technique you can use to get the information you need is to ask questions. All the questions you ask will be trying to find out the *who, what, when, where,* and *why* of your customer's situation as follows:

    Who. Who influences the buying decision, makes the buying decision, signs the checks, establishes product specifications, controls product use, uses the product, is the current supplier, is my competition?

    What. What do you now use, want, need, like about your current situation? Dislike about your current situation? What is current usage, current inventory, current discounts, current price, current budget, expected changes in the future, the status of your proposal, current credit rating? What do you know about my company? Etc.

    When. When will you review, decide, buy, change, want delivery, pay, meet with, cancel, notify, request, try/test, permit, send, begin, use, approve, introduce, sign? Etc.

    Where. Where is product shipped from, used, stored, serviced, inspected? Where is payment, purchase order, documentation? Where did you hear about us? Etc.

    Why. Why do (did) you buy, agree, cancel, choose, say, ask, believe, permit, pay, refuse, prevent? Etc.

3. All the questions you will ask in a selling situation to uncover the who, what, when, where, and why will fall into the

following three categories:

Category A. Asking for facts. You will be questioning customers (or prospects) about the quantifiable aspects of their situation.

- I wonder if you have ever used an outside service like ours?
- Would you mind telling me who your current supplier is?
- Could you tell me how much you are paying now?
- What is your approximate product usage per month?
- Can you initiate a purchase for this quantity, or is headquarters approval required?
- I wonder what you dislike the most about your current supplier?
- To get some idea of the quality you are looking for, would you look at our price categories and pick the one that best suits you?
- Could you tell me what interest rate you are currently paying?
- What other insurance do you have? Or, Do you have other insurance I should know about?
- Approximately how many patients with this problem would you see over a month's time?
- I wonder who is on the purchasing committee?
- Does your accountant recommend that you purchase or lease?
- What do you mean when you say our price is too high?
- What will be your first application of our product?
- I wonder why you haven't used the samples I left you on my last visit.

Category B. Asking for opinion. You will be questioning customers (or prospects) about their judgment and preferences and expectations and fears relative to the selling situation.

- Does the smaller size meet your need for saving space?
- If we could lower your cost, would you consider changing suppliers?
- Do you know anything about my company?
- Will you agree that using a single supplier limits your flexibility when the supplier has production problems?
- What are your concerns about making a change at this time?

- You don't appear to be interested in what we have to offer. I wonder why?
- When do you feel it will be the right time to buy?
- Which model feels more comfortable to you?
- Would you classify yourself as an aggressive or a conservative investor?
- You have agreed that our higher quality will decrease your maintenance costs and our close shipping point would give you an uninterrupted supply. What is it that you want to think about?
- How do you think your boss will react to our proposal?

Category C. Asking for action. You will be asking customers (or prospects) to take actions, such as making choices; giving you permission, approval, information, money, or documents; arranging meetings; trying or testing products; initiating instructions; etc.

- Will you take the two-door or the four-door?
- In what color would you want it?
- Will you eat it here or take it with you?
- Will you finance it through your bank or our credit program?
- Would you like to be billed annually or quarterly?
- How much do you want to pay monthly?
- Should we process this as a lease or a purchase?
- Could you please make an appointment for me to meet your director of engineering?
- On what day next week would you like me to set up the product test?
- In order for us to make a realistic proposal, we will need a printout of your claims experience for the last 24 months. Will you obtain that for me, or do you prefer I get it directly from _____?
- So that there are no surprises, would you be kind enough to call the parts department and tell them I will be arriving this afternoon?
- In order to save you time, if I get your inventory manager on the phone, will you please tell her that my product will be added to your inventory?

- When can I make a presentation to the committee?
- Could you ask your secretary to prepare the requisition now, so I can give it to the purchasing department on my way out?
- Can you give me the name of someone you know whose situation may be similar to yours and could benefit from owning our product?
- If one of my customers would like to speak to a satisfied user of my product, do I have your permission to give the customer your name?

4. The secret to asking the right questions is to know what you want to know before you start asking the questions. Before you make customer contact, ask yourself:
   - What facts about the customer will I need to know?
   - What customer opinions do I need to know?
   - What action do I want the customer to take?

   If you know what you want to know about the customer and know what you want the customer to do, ask any questions that will get the answers you need.

5. Practice your most common questions. Write them down and practice saying them out loud before you try them on customers. If you have good questions, you want to be able to ask them perfectly. If they sound dumb to you, they will sound dumb to the customer.

6. When the customer gives you an answer you don't understand, keep questioning.

7. Make sure that your questioning does not sound like the proverbial third degree to the customer. Couch your questioning in friendly terms such as:
   - I wonder if...
   - Could you please tell me...
   - Would you mind telling me...
   - It would help me to know if...
   - Would you please...

8. Plan a sequence of questions so the easy-to-answer ones come first. Questions that a customer may refuse to answer in the first few minutes of a sales call because they are too

personal or embarrassing may well be answered if they are asked later in the discussion. As you build a relationship with the customer, the answers come more easily.

9. When you ask customers a question, they can no longer be passive or uninvolved in your sales presentation. Sometimes the customers will be slow in responding to your questions. Don't worry about it. They may be slow in responding because they are thinking or because they do not want to answer or do not know the answer to your question. It is normal to get nervous about the silence—but don't answer your own question. If customers don't answer your questions, you will not get the information you need to have to move the sale forward. If you answer your own questions, you will be talking to yourself and the customers will not be involved in the process.

PART 3

How to Uncover More Selling Opportunities

6

They Don't Know Why They Should Do What You Want Them to Do

One discouraging aspect of the selling job is the large number of customers who seem to have no interest in you, your company, or your products. You make your phone calls trying to schedule appointments; you work a full day in the heat, the cold, and the rain trying to tell your sales story—but with little success. You have good products, and you know there are a lot of people out there who should use your products, but you are faced with the frustrating fact that they are not interested. Some of them won't even give you an appointment. Whether you're selling chemicals by the carload or vacuum cleaners door to door, you know you have this problem when you hear:

We don't need any.

I have one. I don't need another one.

We are happy with our current supplier.

The old one seems to be working fine.

We don't want to take on another billing source.

We're trying to limit the number of our suppliers.

These comments make you wonder how those people know they don't need your product if they will not listen to your presentation or even give you an appointment. And what seems even more confusing is when you get an appointment and present your wonderful product, the response you get is:

We will think about it.

We don't want to make a change at this time.

Your product is not right for us.

We decided to stick with our old supplier.

And then there is the killer:

We just bought from someone else.

One reason you get these responses from people you think should be your customers is that *they don't know why they should do what you want them to do.*

From the customer's point of view, they may know that you want them to buy your product or service, but they don't know *why* they should do that. One key to your success is to understand the selling situation from the customer's point of view.

If you don't correctly understand each customer's situation, his responses will not make sense to you and what you do will not make sense to him. Understanding each customer's situation may seem like an unachievable goal because each selling situation in some ways is relative to each customer as a person, the type of business, its size, and level of success. But a closer analysis reveals that in the actual selling situation in regard to a specific product, customers share many commonalities. It is true in life in general that although people are different, when you place them in the same situation, they seem to react in similar ways. For example, people who go to a hospital for an appendectomy are different from one another, but they also have a lot of things in common. If you analyzed the surgical procedures used to remove the appendixes from 1000 patients, you would find that there were not 1000 variations. The procedure would have changed depending upon the patient's age, current health, and past medical history, including allergies and healing problems. If you grouped these patients according to the similarity in the treatment each received, you would find that each type of treatment was administered according to shared commonalities of age or current health, such as high blood pressure or a heart condition, etc.

A similar analysis of the selling process permits us to group different customers in selling situations according to their commonalities. Grouping customers by their commonalities helps us create selling strategies for each group. By using these strategies, we can prepare to sell more successfully by doing the right things at the right time rather than inventing the proverbial wheel for every customer.

As a case in point, let's look at a number of customers who tell you, "We don't need any."

Customer 1

    CUSTOMER: We don't need any.

    YOU: What do you mean by that?

    CUSTOMER: I mean we have enough inventory to last us for the next 12 months.

Conclusion: He doesn't need any *now.*

Customer 2

    CUSTOMER: We don't need any.

    YOU: What do you mean by that?

    CUSTOMER: We are happy with our current supplier.

    YOU: Most of the people we call on are happy with their current supplier. One of the reasons we want to talk to you is because we have developed new product modifications that could cut your maintenance cost by 15 percent. If you could cut 15 percent off your maintenance cost, how much would you save annually?

    CUSTOMER: I don't think you can.

YOU: A lot of customers say that to us on our first call. But if we really could save you 15 percent, would it be worth 15 minutes of your time to learn about it?

CUSTOMER: Yes.

Conclusion: He didn't know his life could be brighter.

Customer 3

CUSTOMER: We don't need any.

YOU: Why do you say that?

CUSTOMER: We have a current supplier and have no reason to change.

YOU: You mean your current supplier is perfect, and nothing he does could be improved?

CUSTOMER: I wouldn't say he's perfect, but we have done a lot of comparisons in the past and selected the vendor we thought was the best.

YOU: If your current supplier could redesign his product and make it perfect, what would it do for you that it does not do now?

CUSTOMER: Well, the cost would be less, it would run longer without breakdowns, and service response time would be half of what it is.

YOU: It sounds as though you are describing the good things our customers say about our product. Could I have 15 minutes of your time to show you why customers say that?

CUSTOMER: Yes.

Conclusion: They need your product (have a problem) but don't know their problem can be solved.

As you can see from these examples, although the customers all said, "We don't need any," each of their situations was different. You will meet a lot of customers whose situation will be similar to one of these three situations. And happily for you, experience has demonstrated that selling actions that succeed with one customer (for example, in situation 1) will also work successfully with other customers in that same situation. This is good news because it means you don't have to invent a totally new selling plan for every customer. But initially you do have to use effective customer situation analysis to be sure you correctly understand each selling situation from the customer's point of view. Incorrect situation analysis will cause you to mislabel these customers and apply the wrong selling strategy. When you learn to use the effective strategy for each major selling situation, you will be a professional ready to face the selling challenge. On a sales call, you will be able to concentrate on collecting the important information you need to know to categorize that customer as a basis for applying your selling strategy.

The chapters that follow present analyses of the most common customer situations and offer specific solutions that will lead you to sales success.

7
They Don't Need What You Are Selling

These customers are now receiving the best product or service for their situation at the best price, with the best credit terms, with the most dependable and convenient delivery and service, or:

They don't *currently* use what you are selling.

OR

They are going out of business.

OR

They have no need for your product or anyone else's product or service different from what they are now receiving.

OR

You really have nothing to offer them.

I once observed a salesperson of alcoholic beverages trying to sell a champagne display to a small liquor store owner whose principal customers bought beer and low-priced wine. The salesperson persisted in trying to sell the display although the owner stated three times that in the 7 years he had been in the business, he had never had a customer ask for champagne.

Solution

1. Don't try to call on all customers. Call on those with the highest potential for buying your product. One way to avoid this situation is to use the profiling process described earlier. Using your profile, collect information about your potential customers to qualify them according to their potential (big gross sales, quick sales, high-profit sales, repeat sales, etc.). Some of the information you need is readily available from newspapers, annual reports, court records, industry activity reports, and other customers. Some information you can get only from direct contact with the customer's organization. This does not mean that you must initially contact the person who makes the buying decision. You can get useful information from receptionists, mail room clerks, shipping and receiving personnel, and others who are or may be users of similar products in that organization.

2. Make sure this situation does not exist merely because the customer says, "I don't need your product." It is up to you to collect enough information about your customer's situation to be certain your product is not needed.

   Customers who really don't need your product could possibly be tricked into believing they have a problem or could benefit from your product. You could lie to them to get them to spend their money for something that they really don't need or that is not as good as you say it is. But that would not be honest or good business. Spending your time trying to sell something to a customer who does not need what you sell is a bad investment of your time.

3. The best salespeople are very effective in qualifying customer potential by phone before making an appointment. This timesaving technique dramatically increases their return on selling time invested.

4. If phone qualification is not possible, classify or qualify each contact as a high- or low-potential customer before you begin your sales presentation.

5. Call on somebody else. Based on estimated sales return from your time invested, the most effective approach might be to schedule your selling time as follows:

   - *Call on first:* Customers who know they have a need and want your product to satisfy that need.
   - *Call on second:* Customers who normally have a need but are not aware that your product can satisfy that need.
   - *Call on third:* Customers who have a need but don't know it, and your product could satisfy that need.

8
They Don't Need Any, Now

When this customer says, "We don't need any," she really means, "We don't need any right now." She uses your type of product or service, but because her need has decreased (business is bad or she has adequate inventory), she doesn't need any right *now*. As frequently happens, the customer may have just bought the product from your competitor. When this happens, you usually call it "the luck of the game." You want to kick yourself for not calling on that customer sooner.

What really hurts, though, is when your competition not only has gotten the sale, but also has "locked up" the customer with long-term purchasing agreements. Even if you get past the receptionist and present your product, you will be wasting your time with this customer today.

Solution

1. If the customer has just purchased a competitive product or is locked into large inventories or long-term contracts, classify her as having current low potential for getting a sale.

2. This customer would only be a current high-potential prospect if:

    a. You had products, buying conditions, and service that will outperform your competition.

    b. You can provide an efficient means of eliminating the customer's current inventory or breaking long-term contracts without a loss to the customer.

3. Don't give up on this customer altogether. Schedule later contacts to learn her usage and ordering pattern so you can schedule your selling activities to coincide with the next reorder cycle. Use your contact time wisely to establish your selling plan and establish rapport. Find out what the level of satisfaction with her current supplier is, what her future needs are, who makes the buying decision, and who influences the buying decision. Your objective is to lay the groundwork so you get the next long-term contract.

9

They Don't Know There Is a Better Way

A customer in this category is aware of his problems, but he is living with them because he believes these problems cannot be reasonably solved (or solved at all). He actually has a need, but he is not aware that your product or anyone's product or service can reasonably fill that need. The term *reasonably* could refer to cost, size, quantity, speed or convenience of delivery, ease of adaptation, safety, training requirements, etc. From the customer's point of view, the world looks like this:

We are using the best we can get for the price.

We have been doing this for 20 years, and we don't think (don't know) there is a better way.

We know the chemical we're using is dangerous, but aren't they all dangerous?

We have tried everything and have found what works best for us.

Yes, there is some danger, but so is walking across the street.

All the products on the market are just about the same.

We have problems with delivery, but doesn't everyone?

Yes, we have to make adjustments when it comes from the vendor, but that's the nature of the beast.

Our telephone costs are high, but we accept that as the price of customer service.

It would be nice to have professional investing advice like the big investors, but I only invest about $1000 per year.

People in this situation present the highest-potential opportunity for you to win at selling if your product or service answers customer needs better than the competition. The greatest selling opportunity always exists when you have a solution to someone else's need.

Solution

1. This customer is open to discussions regarding problems; he knows he has problems. But he is not open to discussing solutions because he thinks there aren't any solutions. That is why you frequently can't get an appointment with this customer. People in this situation believe they know everything there is to know about their situation; they have been trying to solve their problem and believe they have succeeded as best as possible. From their point of view, there is obviously no better solution. People who think they know everything are not closed to discussions; they are merely closed to suggestions. This is an easy sale to make if you have the right product and you do it right. Doing it right means you have to help the customer learn that solutions to his problems do exist. The key word here is *learn*.

2. Your first selling objective is to open up the customer's thinking on the subject. The only way to do that is to sell him on the *idea* that there may be *new* solutions to his problem.

   So, in answer to the customer's question (stated or unstated), "Our problems can't be solved so why should I give you time?" try these approaches:

   - I would like to meet with you to find out if some newly

discovered solutions in the area of [mention your product's area] might be applicable to your situation.

- I would like to meet with you to find out if some solutions used by [cite some organizations with recognizable names] to solve their problems might be applicable to your situation.
- I would like to meet with you to discuss your interest in hearing [fill in the name of a well-known person] discuss [his or her] successes in solving [whatever] problems.
- I would like to meet with you to ask your opinion on some recent (research or information) which may be applicable to your situation.

3. Occasionally you will discover that after doing everything right, there is still one person in the organization who is blocking the buying decision. This may be the person who maintained that the problem could not be solved and if your solution is used, this person will look like a fool. You will have to convert this person to accepting your solution without making him look bad. If you have tried several times but cannot convert this person, evaluate your estimated return from your selling time investment. You may gain more by investing your selling time with another customer where the obstacles are less insurmountable.

10

They Don't Know They Have a Problem

From their viewpoint, these customers don't think they need to buy anything because they are unaware that they have a problem and can see no need for something they don't currently possess. This may sound strange from your point of view, but remember, we are looking at this from the customer's point of view. These people think their world is fine as it is.

To put it another way, these customers are not aware of how much brighter their life could be if they used your product or service; they don't know that by using your product or service that they would gain more reliability, less or easier maintenance, lower cost, better payment terms to improve cash flow, more dependable or convenient delivery, more prestige, more comfort, improved safety or security, etc.

For example, the customer using a copy machine requiring a 40-second warm-up before making copies doesn't know your equipment has a zero warm-up time. The person who owns home fire insurance is not aware that replacement cost is not covered under the existing policy. The person whose savings are invested in conservative bonds paying a solid dividend is not aware that rising inflation is outpacing interest earnings. The retailer buying a product that generates 15 inventory turnovers a year is not aware that your product could produce

20 turnovers a year. The money manager using a software package for account analysis is not aware that your software package could do the same job 20 percent faster.

From their point of view:

Why should I talk to an office furniture salesperson if we don't need any furniture?
The customer doesn't know that different furniture could improve efficiency, add prestige, add physical comfort, decrease office accidents, decrease complaints about back problems, etc.

I have enough insurance to put me into the ground. I don't need any more.
The customer is not aware that burial costs have escalated or that certain insurance can be a tax-free investment.

We have a good supplier and don't need to change.
The customer doesn't know that by changing suppliers she could lower costs, or get better quality for the same price, or get more convenient delivery, or improve cash flow because of lower inventory, or improve reliability.

We are not having any problems with our current phone system. I don't need to waste your time looking at your system.
The customer doesn't know a new system would improve system capacity, or increase the number of functions that can be performed simultaneously and thus obtain greater organization efficiency, or provide better handling of customers, or reduce waiting time for customers calling in for service.

Frequently the person you are trying to sell to may be a purchasing agent buying products for other users in the organization. The purchasing agent may be unaware of the difficulties the users are having with the current competitive product or service. It is not uncommon for a user to be dissatisfied with a product or service even though the complaints do not get back to the actual buyer. From the buyer's point of view, nothing is wrong—there is no need to change. Therefore, buyers don't know why they should talk to you, give you information about themselves, or listen to your product presentation, much less buy your product.

Dealing with a person in this category is very frustrating because you frequently never get a chance to talk to the buyer; it is the secretary or receptionist who delivers the buyer's message, "We don't need any."

But as customers who don't know there is a better way, the customers in this situation present a high-potential opportunity for your sales success if your product or service answers customer needs better than the competition.

Solution

1. The first step to successfully selling to this customer is to uncover or reveal the *customer's* problems or missed opportunities.

   Selling has been defined as finding out what your customer's needs are and doing your best to help satisfy those needs. This definition implies a two-part process. The first part is to *find out what the needs are,* and the second is to *apply your solutions* (product or service). When you do the first part—analyze your customer's needs—you are doing more consulting than selling. This is part of your selling situation analysis. When you don't do the consulting part of your job as well as you should, you will be less successful in doing the selling part of your job. Without knowing a customer's specific need, you will be trying to sell products to people who really don't need them or at best don't know they need them. When they discover that you sold them a product they don't need, you will lose their potential for future sales and begin to build a bad reputation. The needs analysis part of the selling process has proved so critical over the years that writers and trainers have tried to emphasize its importance by renaming the whole selling process as *consultative selling.*

2. A customer in this situation poses a similar problem for you as did the customer in Chapter 9; from your customer's point of view, there is no reason to give you her time. Your first hurdle is to convince her why she should give you some of her time. The secret of success is not to talk about your solu-

tions initially but to convince her that all you want to do is learn more about *her* business (situation). In other words, she is not giving you time to sell her something; she is giving you time to understand more about her situation. This is not a sneaky trick or some other subterfuge. It is a critical part of the successful selling process called *uncovering the customer's needs.* One of the most effective initial customer contacts is the survey approach wherein the salesperson conducts a survey of the customer's situation with the promise to give a survey report to the customer at a later date.

Some successful approaches that have been used to get appointments are as follows:

- I am a new salesperson, and you are in my territory. I would like to meet you and learn something about your organization in the event that I might be of service to you in the future.

- I am new in this industry and [give the name of a person she knows] told me that if I wanted to learn about this business, you would be the person to talk to. (You actually asked the third person whom you should talk to to learn more about the business from the customer's point of view. This is an effective networking technique.)

- I would like to conduct a free survey of your ____ process and give you a report of our findings without any obligation on your part.

- Our company is planning to invest in research to solve problems that are common in your business, and I am contacting experienced individuals who might have some suggestions of areas that might benefit from improvement.

- Because of your experience, I would like to get your opinion on the best way to sell our new product.

- I am looking for an objective opinion about one of our products, and although you probably don't need it, I wonder if you would be kind enough to look at it and evaluate it from an objective point of view.

- Our market research has discovered that ____ percent of the people in your situation have [state a problem or loss] and are not aware of it. I would be willing to conduct a free analysis of your situation to find out if you are in that ____ percent category.

3. It's very important not to lie to the customer or the staff to get an appointment. If you lie to get the appointment, why should the customer believe you are telling the truth when you talk about your product?

4. In some situations it's extremely difficult to make contact with the decision maker. When that's the case, use the "end-run" approach by calling on lower-level people in the organization to initially collect information about their needs. Lower-level people are usually easier to get to meet. They may be surprised that you want to meet with them, but they will like the attention and will usually give you a lot of information. You can use the information you collect to create a report you can use as an introduction to the decision maker. Frequently you can get the lower-level people to make an appointment for you with the decision maker.

5. Your CAO for your first sales call is for the customer to fully describe his needs. Unless your product can be sold in one sales call, don't get into your product presentation on this initial contact. The danger is that you may not learn as much as you need to know and your product presentation will be less effective. Even if you had to mention some of your product benefits to get the appointment with the customer, devote your first call to uncovering needs.

6. When you have uncovered or identified the customer's needs, you can plan your sales strategy (how many calls will it take) and sales presentation (CAO and planned actions for each sales call). With this customer, the pivotal point for getting the sale will be the customer's agreement that he has a need (to solve a problem or make his life brighter). If you have done your customer needs analysis correctly, at this point you will be talking about the customer's world from his point of view. He will know why he should talk to you.

11

They Don't Know Why They Should Buy What You Are Selling

A customer in this situation knows he has a problem and believes it could be solved, but he does not think that your product will solve his problem or brighten his life. This is one of the biggest obstacles you will have to overcome to succeed in selling. This is not a case of the customer not knowing that your organization provides the needed product or service. This situation occurs after you have made your product presentation, but you did not convince the customer why he should own your product. You didn't do your job.

Unfortunately for you and all other salespeople, customers rarely say, "You didn't convince me why I should buy your product." Their responses are usually more subtle. They leave you mystified with such comments as:

We are not ready to make a decision right now.

You have a good product, but we don't think it's right for us at this time.

You have a good product, but we want to see what else is available.

It is nice, but I would like to think about it.

These people need a product like yours. They just don't know why they should buy your product versus someone else's product.

Two Main Reasons for Customers' Doubts

One big question in every customer's mind when you are presenting your product is, "Why should I buy this product?" Rarely does the customer ask it out loud, but it must be answered to the customer's satisfaction to make the sale. Many salespeople fail because they do not answer customers' questions *to the customers' satisfaction.* There are two main reasons for this selling failure.

Confusing Features and Benefits

The first reason, which is the most common but the easiest to solve, is the salesperson's confusion between:

1. *Features:* How *good* the product is

and

2. *Benefits:* How the customer's life will *become brighter* from owning the product

In spite of all the selling literature available emphasizing "benefit selling," it is surprising that so many salespeople confuse the two. When you describe the quality of your product, the way it is made, its accuracy, its use of special materials, its sturdy construction, the millions of dollars your organization has invested in perfecting it, and the total organization's commitment to producing the perfect product, you are only answering the customer's question, "How good is your product?" You are describing product *features* that never change for your product unless you change how you design, construct, or deliver your product or service. When you describe the features of your product, you are describing to the customer why you are selling that product.

When you describe customer *benefits*, you are answering the customer's question—"How will I benefit from owning your product?" and dealing exclusively with how your product will make the *customer's* life brighter. These *benefits*, which are totally customer-oriented, will either solve a customer's problems or add pleasure the customer never had before. These benefits can be as simple as less waiting time for a copy machine to warm up before producing copies, less perspiration because of all-cotton fabrics, lower maintenance costs because of fewer breakdowns, improved customer image, fewer billing sources because of your broad product line, or reduced inventory because of your more frequent deliveries. When you talk about benefits, you are describing to the customer why he or she should own your product. Unfortunately, the importance of any benefit varies according to a customer's specific need. All benefits do not apply to all customers, and all customers do not consider any single benefit with equal desirability.

The sales vice president of a company selling lubrication to manufacturers complained to me that a video developed by the sales department to sell a new lubricant was not helping sales of the new product. He said that although the 5-minute video was quite impressive in demonstrating how the new lubricant could reduce maintenance costs by as much as 20 percent, the salespeople were having difficulty getting manufacturing managers and engineers to view the video. When I traveled with his salespeople to observe actual sales calls, the problem was quite evident. The salespeople were asking customers if they would like to see a 5-minute video on a new lubricant. Most of the customers said "no," they didn't have the time. Obviously, the prospect of watching a 5-minute video about lubricants did not project many benefits to these customers. But when I convinced the salespeople not to mention the video first but instead to ask customers, "Would you like to learn how to reduce machine maintenance costs by 20 percent?" all the customers said "yes" and watched the video. The crucial point is that "showing the video" was what was important to the salespeople, but "learning something" (from the video) was what was important to the customers. Incidentally, sales of the new lubricant also increased. Every year people purchase millions of light bulbs, not because they want light bulbs, but because they want light. It is the benefits of owning something which causes the buying.

Both features and benefits are important in selling, but salespeople frequently make the mistake of believing that when they are talking about one, they are, in fact, talking about the other, or that the two are interchangeable. They are, however, distinctly different and are definitely not interchangeable.

The Communication Traps

The second reason why salespeople fail in this situation is because they communicate badly. Below are some of the traps you can fall into:

1. You don't talk about benefits at all. You know this happened when you hear, "It looks good, but we don't need it."

2. You talk about the benefits of owning the product, but the benefits you describe are not related to this customer. Perhaps this customer's primary interest in your equipment is convenience of operation and not costs, but you describe cost-saving benefits and don't mention convenience.

   I recently observed a good example of this when making sales calls with a sales representative selling pharmaceuticals to doctors. On the three previous sales calls earlier that day, the doctors had raised questions about the price of the product because their patients often complained about the high price of antibiotics. On this sales call, the first thing the sales representative mentioned to the doctor was the low price of the product she was selling. The doctor's response was, "I don't care about price. I only care about saving patients' lives. When patients complain to me about price, I always tell them, "It's cheaper than a funeral, so stop complaining." In this situation, the sales representative was presenting information she thought was important; unfortunately, it was not important to that customer. She could have asked, "Is price a concern for you, doctor?" and responded to the answer.

3. You talk about benefits, but the customer doesn't hear what you are saying because you lost her attention. When you make a sales presentation, the customer is exposed to a lot of information in a short period of time. You present this information because all of it is necessary to get the customer to make a buying decision. Sometimes, though, the customer misses some of your important points, gets confused, or cannot relate all of the information you presented. The same thing happens when someone finishes telling a long humorous story with lots of characters and critical incidents in the plot and no one laughs. We could blame the listener for having no sense of humor, but more likely he got lost along the way. Sometimes you know your customer got lost along the way when you lose eye contact with him, when he fiddles with other work papers, or when he asks totally unrelated questions when you finish your statement. But frequently you only know this happened when you hear, "It is not what we are looking for."

4. You talk about benefits and the customer hears what you're talking about, but doesn't understand what you're saying because your sentence structure is too complicated, or because you speak too fast or you mumble. I observed one salesperson say "you know" twenty-seven times to the customer in a 20-minute sales presentation. You can assume that you have lost the customer when he asks you to explain what you just explained; he seems to have fallen asleep with open eyes; he says, "I'm not sure we need it"; or he asks you to leave some literature to read about your product.

You know that your product or service could help the customer, but your problem is that the customer does not know that (yet).

Solution

1. Accept the fact that when the customer says "We don't need any," it is not the end of the selling process; it is the beginning of the selling process. Start asking questions to validate that comment. A good starter is "I wonder why," or "Can you tell me why," or "What do you mean?"

2. Customers frequently do not clearly describe their willingness to buy or decision not to buy. They, in fact, frequently misclassify themselves. The person who says "I don't need any" is usually misinformed. It is up to you to collect enough information to correctly classify the situation.

3. Pay attention to the elements in each customer's situation that influence her decisions. To understand why customers do or don't do what you want them to do, interpret the world from their point of view, not from your point of view. Always keep in mind that they don't see it from your point of view—and their point of view is the only important one for getting or losing the sale.

4. Recognize that people buy things because of the benefits they expect to gain from owning them. Avoid the trap of presenting all features and all benefits to all customers whether they need them or not. Don't waste your time putting potential customers to sleep and losing sales.

5. Become an expert on the features and benefits of your product or service. Recognize that all customers buying the same product are not the same. They don't have the same needs; they don't derive the same benefits from the same product. Frequently, one product feature can provide several different benefits. For example, if the design of your equipment makes the product small in size and light in weight, the benefits could be:

a. It's easy to carry.
b. It needs less storage space.
c. It may be operated as a desktop unit so you don't need a separate stand.

If you are presenting this product to a customer who must lift the product and he weighs 100 pounds, the primary feature would be that it is light in weight. If you are presenting your product to an average-size customer who is working in a limited space, he might have no interest in its light weight but would see great benefit in saving space.

If one of the features of your company's service is that you make frequent deliveries of small amounts of product, in contrast with the competition, which delivers large amounts infrequently, the benefits from that single feature could be reduction in inventory, less storage space required, fresher product, lower cost of inventory, and better control of cash flow. However, improved cash flow would not be a benefit to a customer having no cash flow problems, and saving storage space would not be a benefit to a customer having no storage space problems.

Although a large number of people need a specific product, they may not all need the same quality of product. In other words, they all don't need a perfect product and, therefore, don't see the need for spending money for a perfect product. For example, if you need a handsaw to occasionally cut wood around the house, you would not purchase a handsaw of the same quality as purchased by a carpenter or cabinetmaker. These craftsmen use a saw as a tool every day. You only need a saw for occasional work. What you buy would not be of good enough quality for a carpenter, and what the carpenter buys would be of better quality than you need. The differences between needs in this example appear obvious. It is up to you to collect enough information so your customer's needs are also obvious to you.

6. Make up a list of all the features of each product you sell. Make up a list of all the possible customer benefits that can be gained from each feature. Using a list of your customers (or potential customers), group customers according to

things they share in common (size, volume of usage, type of business, current competitive product used, product application, etc.). Make up a list of needs that each group has in common. Match each group to your list of features and benefits to identify which features and benefits apply to each group's needs.

7. If you have properly grouped your customers by commonality of business and needs, you can forecast their needs in order to plan your presentation. But use questioning techniques to get customers to *tell you* what they need. When they tell you their needs, you don't have to guess. You can ask:

   - What don't you like about your present product?
   - What problems are you having with your present product?
   - Since you are now using product X, are you having the same problem others have told about, such as _____ ?
   - If you could send your current product back to the factory and make it perfect, what would it do that it does not do now?
   - If you could wave a magic wand and make your current product perfect, what would you wish for?

8. To keep your presentations benefit-oriented, follow the rule that you don't talk about a product feature unless you mention the benefit(s) that the customer gains from that feature.

9. To make sure the benefits you mentioned are important to your customer, ask the customer after presenting each one if that benefit is [important, useful, helpful, or valuable] to him or solves the [problem, need] he previously mentioned.

10. The only way to avoid mumbling, talking too fast, or using confusing sentences is to plan what you are going to say and *practice* it. Pay attention to the "show business" part of selling. Practice, practice, and practice until you don't have to think about the words, the emphasis, the pauses and voice modulations; you will be free to concentrate on what the customer says and does.

11. Ask questions throughout your presentation to make sure you don't lose your customer's interest. Questions will veri-

fy that your customer understands your message, and, more importantly, will reveal the changes in opinion you are trying to achieve. Examples of questions include:

- Do you see how compounding the interest gives you more total earnings over the same period of time?
- Do you agree that our special counter display will generate more impulse buying?
- Do you agree that our co-op advertising program has the potential of increasing your walk-in traffic?
- Do you agree that a 25 percent decrease in equipment downtime will more than make up for the slightly higher initial tool cost?
- On the basis of these statistics, have I proved to your satisfaction that it is safer than what you are now using?

PART 4

If It's Just Talk, You Won't Get the Sale

12

They Don't Enjoy Talking to You

There are customers, or more correctly potential customers, who say that they will not see any salespeople. But some who say that do give appointments to some salespeople and even go out to lunch with them. Apparently, what they mean is that they will not meet with you. This can be even more frustrating if you have met the customer once, but you can't get a second appointment. You try to do everything right: You take baths. You dress nice. You use breath freshener. You are polite. But you still do not get the appointment. When you learn that this customer buys the products you sell from the competition, it goes beyond disappointment. It hurts you in your wallet. You may conclude that these customers are weird or that they don't like you, and in either case you could be right. But there might be something happening here that you don't understand.

Let's take a look at it from the customer's point of view. All relationships between customers and salespeople function on two levels: the social level and the business level. The business level includes all aspects of the customer's business as related to your business products and services. The social level deals with you and the customer on a personal basis: how the customer feels about you as a person, the way you act, the way you talk, and in general something you could call friendliness.

In the old days when a traveling salesman made his rounds by train and horseback, his arrival in the customer's office was a notable and welcomed occasion. On his 1- to 3-month field trips, he had seen more sights and visited more places than his customers, been exposed to many and varied experiences, and had a lot of interesting things to talk about. He had news; not only did he know about what other customers in the same business were doing, but he also knew a lot of human interest stories—the kind of stories that people who follow a heavy and continuous traveling schedule are prone to pick up. The traveling salesman was an entertainer without trying to be one and usually had no trouble getting to see customers because he was an interesting personality.

From the customer's point of view, it was an interesting day when the out-of-town salesman arrived from the big city; the customer was going to learn something, as well as hear some funny and sad stories, whether or not they were true. The stereotype of the back-slapping, joke-telling salesperson came from a time in history when that's what the salesperson was, a traveling celebrity. Most salespeople were interesting people to talk to, on a social level as well as on a business level.

Since we have become a more sophisticated society, the news and entertainment media now widely disseminate those stories and rumors that once were the unique currency of the traveling salesman. Also, the shrinking of territories and the proliferation of the number of salespeople have resulted in salespeople not being as interesting as they used to be. The modern emphasis on the technical approach to selling has even generated an avoidance of the stereotypical "good-time Charlie" salesperson to the extent that a lot of salespeople don't pay any attention to the social aspects of the sales call. We've moved away from what appeared to be a totally social relationship with little selling going on to today's concentration on mostly selling with little emphasis on the social relationship.

I recently spent the day observing sales calls with a salesperson who had just returned from a trip to Acapulco he had won as first prize in a sales contest. He won the contest by telling his customers about the contest and getting them to stock more of his product in 30 days than anybody else in his region. As we visited 10 of his customers that day, he told me that most of them were a big help in his winning the trip because they bought a lot of merchandise during the contest period. I noticed that he didn't mention Acapulco or thank even one of the customers whose buying action had won him his trip. When I mentioned that to him at the end of the day, he became shocked and starry-eyed and said, "Gee, I guess I should have done that." I also asked him if he had sent greeting cards from Acapulco to these customers who had in fact sent him there, thanking them for their efforts. He said he hadn't done that either, but he thought it would have been a good idea. You might wonder what these customers will do the next time he tells them he needs their business so he can win a contest.

If They Don't Like You, They Won't Like Your Product

I've had salespeople tell me that they do not use social chitchat with the staff or customers and do not tell funny stories because they are trying to be professional. My response was that if they do not try to chitchat and use some humor, they are being unprofessional because they are avoiding an important aspect of the selling situation. These same salespeople go even one step further and fail to develop any interest in the customer as a person. Once, when sitting in the lobby with a salesperson waiting to see a customer, I noticed seven paintings on the wall which seemed rather amateurish. When I asked the salesperson if he knew who painted them, he said he did not know. When we eventually got in to see the customer, the salesperson asked him about the paintings. The customer said that they were painted by his son. The salesperson had not previously known that and yet he had been calling on that customer for 3 years.

When traveling with another salesperson, we called on a customer who had a picture of himself shaking hands with the President of the United States on his office wall. After the call, when I asked the salesperson what the customer's relationship was with the President, the salesperson didn't even know what picture I was talking about. These salespeople knew a lot about their product and the customer's type of business, but they didn't know anything about the customer as a person and had no person-to-person or social relationship with that customer.

If a customer has the choice of talking to one of two salespeople selling highly similar products, he will choose to spend time with the salesperson having the most positive social relationship with the customer. If one salesperson has a social relationship and you do not, the customer's choice is an easy one. From the customer's point of view, talking to you is not enjoyable, and so why should he give you his time.

A salesperson's inability to get time in front of customers is sometimes due to a lack of a social relationship, as well as to a bad social relationship. If we could secretly put a tape recorder in your customer's office to hear what that customer says when you call for an appointment or arrive for a sales call, is this what we would hear?

Oh God, not him. He puts you to sleep.

Not today. I don't need a lecture on how wonderful her company is.

All he does is argue.

Tell her to leave her literature. I can't waste time with her.

This guy is dull, dull, dull!

She knows her product, but she never lets you finish a sentence.

Or would you hear the customer say:

Hey, that's a nice surprise. Send him in.

I'm looking forward to seeing her. I have some questions to ask.

It's always good talking to him. When can he come in to see me?

It's always a pleasure talking to him. He brightens my day.

I was just thinking about her. She knows more about our problems than anybody else. When can she come in to see me?

It's always pleasant to talk to him.

Sometimes meeting with you is not pleasant for the customer because of your personal habits. You may in fact not smell nice, or perhaps you have bad breath; or you may do things that are offensive to the customer, for example:

Smoking

Putting your materials on the customer's desk without requesting permission

Interrupting the customer when she is speaking

Using statements that are offensive, such as "You're wrong" or "You don't know what you're talking about"

Wearing an overpowering cologne or perfume

Shaking your head "no" while the customer is trying to explain his point of view

Frowning or rolling your eyes and grimacing, denoting a negative response to what the customer is saying

The customer may not want to have lunch with you because you have bad table manners, or you overeat, or you overdrink, or you're too boisterous or too rude to waiters while you play the "big wheel" in restaurants.

So far we're merely talking about getting time to be able to sell the customer. But if you don't know it already, understand that a large percentage of sales are made or lost according to how much the customer likes the salesperson. If the final decision is between two products or services with little or no product differentiation, the buying decision will go to the person the customer likes best. Unfortunately, customers rarely announce that they are buying a product because they like the salesperson. They will give other reasons to support their buying decision, such as:

I have more confidence in this person.

They seem to be more in tune with our needs.

The chemistry seems to be better.

They seem more like our kind of people.

But as important as the social relationship is as part of the selling process, it is not the sole reason why customers give you their time or buy your products. In the old days, the traveling salesman had a very broad perspective of the industry within which he was selling and could talk knowledgeably about problems, solutions, and new trends in that industry. One benefit of listening to a traveling salesman was that he gave out helpful information the customer would not get any other way. Today, customers continue to have needs, problems to be solved, or benefits to be gained, and they expect salespeople to help them by bringing knowledge to the meeting. So from the customer's point of view, she would also not enjoy talking to you if you were not knowledgeable in your job. Perhaps we would hear this on the hidden tape recorder:

I don't have time today to hold his hand.

I don't have time to train another sales rep today.

I don't run a training school for these people. I wish they would send somebody who can give me answers.

Tell her to come back in about 5 years when she knows as much about her products as I do.

Obviously, these salespeople are not considered by the customer as a source of information or solutions. You could be that salesperson if you don't know your product line, if you don't know your pricing, if you don't know the details of the customer's situation, or if you don't know how competitive products compare with yours. You would be wasting the customer's time. From the customer's point of view, if her life can't get brighter by talking to you today, then why should she spend her time talking to you. The answer is she shouldn't and won't.

Solution

1. Accept the fact that the social or personal relationship is an important part of the effective selling process and you must pay attention to it or lose sales. Your contacts with cus-

tomers are similar to those of a doctor's contacts with patients. The purpose of a doctor's contact with a patient is to provide advice and treatment to make the patient's life brighter. The salesperson tries to provide advice or services to customers to make their lives brighter. Doctors must collect information from a patient to understand as much as possible about that patient's situation to be certain the treatment and advice are the most effective for that patient's situation. Salespeople must do the same with a customer to be certain the recommended product or service is the best for that customer's situation. The amount of time doctors have available for each patient is limited and must be planned and controlled to provide optimum assistance to large numbers of patients. Similarly, your selling time is limited. In some ways, your time constraints are worse than those facing doctors. As you know, patients will spend a lot of time waiting to see a doctor who may be as much as an hour behind schedule. But customers don't do that; sometimes they don't even see you when you are on time for your appointment. But even with the pressure of providing optimum treatment in minimum time, doctors spend some time establishing rapport.

They don't do that merely to be a nice person. They create a friendly relationship to support the medical relationship. This relaxes the patient, decreases apprehensions, and generates a feeling of trust so that the patient will talk more freely, be more cooperative, and have positive expectations about the treatment. Your goals for using social conversations to establish rapport with your customer are similar. You want to relax the customer, decrease apprehensions, and generate a feeling of trust in you so the customer will talk freely, be more cooperative, and have positive expectations about your relationship.

Doctors have admitted to me that patients are patients and not their friends. This does not mean that doctors don't like people, or that their patients are not nice people, or that some patients don't occasionally become friends, or that a friend may never become a patient. It means that because doctors see a lot of patients briefly each day in a professional circumstance, they concentrate on the patient's medical circumstance, not on friendship. The more minutes the doctor devotes to friendship on one patient, the fewer minutes available for treatment for other patients. This does not mean that the doctor is unfriendly or cannot talk in a friendly way while administering treatment. It merely means that the objective of the meeting between doctor and patient is not friendship; it is improved health for the patient.

As a salesperson, you must devote selling time to getting to know your customers, establishing rapport, and acting in a friendly manner. But the objective of this activity is not to make friends; it is to establish a basis for a sale. It is easy to be friendly with people you like, but part of your professional behavior as a salesperson is to act friendly with your customers whether or not you like them. If you do this, some of your customers will become your friends (accidentally). You might think it is hard to act friendly when you don't feel like it, and you are correct. Doing that and many other things you have to do to be successful in selling are hard to do. They are not impossible, just hard to do. But this is no different from other activities that require skill and practice to be successful. It is part of acting professional.

2. You are the one who must initiate social discussions to establish rapport. You know you have rapport when the customer is talking about subjects of interest to the customer. This could be pleasant things from the customer's point of view, or even things the customer wants to complain about. You must learn about the customer's interests, such as hobbies, sports, family relationships, changes in his business world, important dates like birthdays and anniversaries, the places he goes on vacation, the kind of car he drives. Don't try to get all this information on the first call or it will sound like an interrogation.

3. Use other sources to learn about your customer: talk to staff people; read the local newspapers and be observant. Look for changes around her place of business—a new parking lot, new office furniture, new decorations, increase or decrease in staff, etc.

4. Before each sales call ask yourself, "What can I do that will make this a pleasant event for the customer?" I know one salesperson who always carries individually wrapped hard candy and offers one to each customer as soon as they meet. He has no trouble seeing customers, and many of them ask for their favorite flavor even before they say hello.

   You can plan to bring things that may be of only social interest to the customer. When reading magazines and newspapers, you should be clipping items that you know are of interest to each of your customers. For example, if the customer is interested in horse breeding, bring information you've extracted from newspapers or magazines about horse breeding.

   The friendly relationship may encompass only a friendly hello, a smile, an appropriate handshake (firm in the United States, not firm in France), and a minute or two of discussion.

5. Check your personal hygiene and appearance. Don't wear what you want to wear; wear what you think the customer will think is appropriate for the selling situation. Get some feedback from somebody who won't lie to you about your breath and body odor and your table manners.

6. Learn everything you need to know about the customer's situation. If the customer feels that you do not understand her business, she has no reason to talk to you.

7. Practice using effective communication skills with your customers.
   a. Smile a lot.
   b. Maintain eye contact.
   c. Acknowledge your customer's comments (by interjecting "yes," "uh huh," "hmm," "that's interesting").
   d. Don't interrupt customers when they speak to you.
   e. When customers are speaking, don't shake your head "no" or make negative grimaces or frown because you disagree.
   f. Don't laugh at the customer's problems or belittle him, his business, or his staff. Avoid negative responses, such as

"You are wrong," or "You don't know what you're talking about," or "You people are in the dark ages," or "You people are unsophisticated," or "You people are small time," or "You people are too monolithic."

8. Be friendly but be respectful to customers and their staff. Don't make the mistake of trying to be a stand-up comedian slapping people on the back. That will also close the door to you.

9. Become an expert in your products. Know everything there is to know about your products so that you can answer all your customer's questions.

    Keep track of how many times on a sales call you say, "I don't know," or "I'll get back to you," or "I'll check on that," when the customer asks you a question. If you say things like that more than once or twice, it means you don't know your products as well as you should. Go back and study.

    Know about your competitor's product and how they compare in detail to yours.

10. Like the old-time traveling salesman, be a source of information for your customers by being current in your knowledge of his or her industry.

11. Assume that every time you say hello to a customer, he or she will say, "What's new?" and be prepared to answer that question. Before you contact the customer, ask yourself what is it I can tell the customer today that is new or different from what we talked about the last time.

12. Maintain your friendly relationship with each customer between your visits by sending greeting cards, friendly notes, news clippings, etc. One salesperson (whose product line had nothing to do with trucks), while reading *Truck Stop World Magazine*, discovered that a potential customer who owned a truck stop had won an award. The salesperson managed to visit and congratulate the man even before the man's mother congratulated him.

13. Avoid romantic and/or sexual relationships with customers and members of their staff.

13

They Don't Know What You Want Them to Do

Unbelievable as it may seem, this is a most common reason for not making a sale. This doesn't mean that customers don't know that you want them to buy something; they certainly know that. But they don't know specifically what it is you want them to do so that the sale will move forward. This could be one of your customers who is always willing to see you, gives you time, and listens to your presentation, but the sale never happens. Or what's even worse, perhaps the customer agrees to buy your product and agrees to do things to initiate that purchase but never gets around to doing them. Frequent complaints I hear from salespeople are:

The order didn't go through because he didn't clear it with the purchasing committee.

The equipment was never delivered because she didn't file for her government license to operate it.

He keeps telling me he'll give us some of his business, but nothing ever happens.

I delivered the samples to her 6 months ago and as of today she hasn't used them.

He keeps asking for literature, but I never get the order.

> She is always willing to give you her time, but she never buys anything.

> I told him a few months ago I want to meet the director of engineering, and I'm still waiting for that to happen.

> She told me the vice president is the one who makes the buying decision, but she hasn't made the move to introduce me.

Then there is the saddest one of all:

> I have been calling on him for 3 months, and today I found out he purchased the same service from someone else.

A few years ago, one of my newly acquired associates was complaining to me about a client who bought consulting services from a competitive consulting company, and he couldn't understand why. He told me that he had been calling on that client for several months and had built up what he thought was a solid relationship. He described in detail how he had worked for several months with this client, getting to more fully understand his problems, as well as formulating possible solutions. There was some customer resistance because the client had never before purchased consulting services. But he felt that the relationship was progressing and that he eventually would get the client's business. But to his surprise, when he contacted the client the previous day, the client announced that he had purchased the consulting services from someone else.

I told the frustrated associate the best way to find out why he lost the sale was to go back and ask the customer that question. The consultant met with the client 2 days later, and this is how he described the conversation.

CONSULTANT: Thanks for fitting me into your schedule, John. We have had several discussions over the last 3 months about training your managers, and I thought we were in the formulating stages for setting up a program for you. I was surprised to hear early this week that you purchased the training service from someone else, and I was wondering why.

CUSTOMER: Well, the other consultant is with a good company, and his services are about equal to yours, and they seem ready to provide the training now without any delay. It looks like we'll be able to complete those programs before the first of the year.

CONSULTANT: Well, we would have been able to do the same thing for you, John.

CUSTOMER: I wasn't aware of that. You and I never discussed dates, and I was under the impression that you folks were so busy with your *Fortune* 500 clients that you wouldn't be able to get to me until after the first of the year.

CONSULTANT: Well, you never told me that you wanted to conduct that training so soon.

CUSTOMER: I assumed that you understood that we didn't want to live forever with our management training problem, and you didn't mention anything about schedule dates for the training.

The rest of the discussion was merely traveling music to help the consultant out the door. What is obvious from this conversation is that there were no specific dates discussed and the salesperson never asked specifically for the business (the closing question). He was selling, selling, selling, but never asked the customer to *buy*. At the top of the list of reasons why salespeople fail is "they don't ask the customer to take action; they don't close the sale."

It is easy to label a customer as dumb or lazy or passive or uncooperative because he or she does not take the obvious actions to advance the sale. The problem is that what may seem obvious to us as salespeople is not obvious to the customer. They simply don't know specifically what it is you want them to do. Of course, the selling job would be a lot easier if customers would only realize that their only purpose on earth is to serve us salespeople. Things would go a lot easier like this:

CUSTOMER: Gee, you have a nice product. I think we can use that. What would you like me to do?

SALESPERSON: I would like you to buy my product.

CUSTOMER: How many should I buy?

SALESPERSON: A dozen would do.

CUSTOMER: When would you like to deliver those?

SALESPERSON: The first of next month.

CUSTOMER: Do you want me to sign anything?

SALESPERSON: Yes, my order blank, and I need a purchase order number.

CUSTOMER: I don't have one. Would you like to wait while I call purchasing to get one for you?

SALESPERSON: Yes.

CUSTOMER: Is there anything else you need?

SALESPERSON: Yes, I need a credit statement filled out.

CUSTOMER: Do you want me to fill that out while you wait, or can I mail it to you?

SALESPERSON: You can mail it to me.

CUSTOMER: When do I have to mail it so you will get it in time to have my order shipped on time?

SALESPERSON: I will need that by Friday.

CUSTOMER: Is there anything else you need?

SALESPERSON: Yes, I need your specifications from your engineering department.

CUSTOMER: Would you like me to call and make an appointment right now so you can meet with my engineering manager?

SALESPERSON: Yes, thank you.

CUSTOMER: When would you like to meet with the engineering manager?

SALESPERSON: How about tomorrow?

CUSTOMER: What time tomorrow would be convenient for you?

SALESPERSON: In the afternoon.

CUSTOMER: What time in the afternoon?

If you have never sold before, this conversation may seem reasonable to you, but believe me, it is dreamland; it doesn't happen that way. Customers are not here to serve salespeople; we are here to serve customers. In general, customers are willing to cooperate with us. The problem is that we don't tell them exactly what it is we want them to do and/or when we need it done. For example:

We ask a customer to try our sample to demonstrate that the product will work for her and we deliver our sample, but we never ask the customer what specific day the sample will be used.

We want the customer to introduce us to the director of engineering, but we never ask him to actually schedule a specific appointment to meet the director.

We want the customer to apply for her federal license, but we never ask her to fill out a specific form to be mailed on any specific date.

Sometimes we only hint about what we want because we don't want to pressure the customer. We need a copy of an updated credit report by a specific date in order to submit the customer's order, but we don't ask for that. Instead we say, "Of course we will need an updated credit report."

When I ask salespeople why they don't ask customers for what they want, the most common answer is, "I don't want to get pushy or pressure the customer," or "I don't want to alienate the customer because I want to be able to call on her again." Some salespeople don't ask for what they want from the customer on a sales call because they don't know how to phrase it; they don't practice ahead of time.

But our consulting analysis of this common "not-asking" problem reveals an even bigger reason: most salespeople don't know specifically what they want the customer to do. So they ask general or dumb questions, such as "Can we have your business?" or "Will you think about it?"

This is less of a problem for salespeople selling a one-sales-call product, where the desired customer action is for the customer to give up his money. Under these conditions, letting the customer know what you want becomes quite easy:

How many do you want?

Will you eat it here or take it with you?

Cash, credit card, or personal check?

Do you want a service contract?

As mentioned in Chapter 3, "Selling Is the Management of Buying," when you're selling a product that requires multiple sales calls, you know what you want the customer to do on the last call, which is to give you his or her money or a purchase order. But, unfortunately, you don't know what you want the customer to do on the prior calls. If you're trying to sell a group insurance plan, the objective on the first or second call is to get a computer printout of all employees and their ages and incomes. If you only tell the customer, "I need a computer printout of all the employees in your current insurance group," you may get it but not as soon as you need it. Or the customer might even assume you intend to get that printout from someone else in the organization and therefore do nothing.

These situations that salespeople typically describe as customer "resistance to buying" are more correctly the salesperson's "resistance to selling."

Solution

1. View your selling activities as getting the customer ready to buy. When you do your needs analysis, helping the customer uncover his problems and needs, you are getting him to understand all the ramifications of these problems—the cost of not fixing them (the pain, the money, the loss of profits, the loss of business, the unpleasantness and lack of success). This is getting the customer to come to the conclusion, "Yeah, I don't like this." Sometimes customers will come to you already saying "I don't like this," and that may be the reason why they called your company in the first place.

   The second part of getting a customer ready to buy is the presentation of alternative solutions. You present features and benefits to help the customer understand that there are solutions to problems he wants to eliminate or to help brighten his life. You do all the hard work of letting him know he has to spend money and effort to change what he is now doing to make this problem go away. So the customer finally concludes, "Yes, I see I do have to change. I do have to spend money in order to make this problem go away."

The customer is now ready to buy. Sometimes the customers who seem to be resisting the most are being moved slowly but surely through the "getting-ready-to-buy process."

But once the customer arrives at the state of "I'm ready to buy," there is no rule that says he must buy your product unless you have the only product in the world to satisfy that customer's need or desire. Unfortunately, there are a lot of products in the world that do about the same job reasonably well. If you get a customer to the ready state and don't ask him to take action (the closing question), the next salesperson who asks for the business is going to get it. You did all the hard work, but somebody else asked the closing question and got the sale.

2. Before you walk into the call, know what it is you want the customer to do and when you want her to do it.

3. Once you know what you want the customer to do, write out how you're going to ask for it.

   Phrase what you're going to ask in a way you think is most effective, and practice how and when you're going to ask it. Some ways of saying things are better than others. For example, "Could you make an appointment for me to meet the vice president?" is not as effective as "I have some free time this week. Would you please call the vice president and see if she can fit me into her schedule Thursday or Friday?"

4. If the customer is supposed to do something to advance the sale after you leave, validate that the customer knows what it is he is supposed to do. Ask, "Just to keep it straight in my mind, I wonder if we could take a minute to review what it is I'm supposed to do." And then state specifically what it is you're supposed to do. Then say, "Could you please review for me what is it you're going to do?"

5. If something must be done to advance the sale and you can do it, don't ask the customer to do it. For example, if you want some information by phone next week, don't ask the customer to call you; you call the customer. Relying on the customer could mean some percentage of the time she will not do it and you will lose.

6. It is not enough to tell the customer you need something. You have to ask for exactly what you want. For example:

   - What is the name of the person who would prepare this kind of printout?
   - Could you do me a favor and call her now to see if it would be convenient for us to meet now to discuss what we will need on the printout?
   - How soon will I be able to pick up the printout?
   - Could you call the vice president's secretary and ask him what day this week would be convenient for us to meet?
   - If I deliver the samples to you this week, what day would you be using them?
   - I will be in the area on Thursday morning. Can you complete the credit report by then so I can pick it up around noontime?
   - We have a holiday coming up. Would you be able to do that before the holiday?

7. Don't be afraid to ask customers your closing questions. Customers don't get mad when you help them buy products they need, but they do get mad when you waste their time. Besides, whether or not the customers are mad at you, if the customers don't buy your products, why do you want to see them again?

PART 5

How to Get More Sales by Overcoming Customers' Fears

14
They Are
Afraid to Buy

One common experience all salespeople share is calling on a customer who never says "no" but who also never says "yes." The customer welcomes you with open arms, acts friendly, gives you free coffee, and shares information with you. However, when you ask for the order, he says:

We don't want to rush this.

We are still thinking about it.

We want to make sure it is the right decision for us.

We want to make sure it is the right time.

From your point of view, you have done everything you know how to do, and yet the customer will not make a decision. You are frustrated because he keeps stalling. When I discuss this problem with sales reps, they tell me:

He says he likes my product, but I can't get him to make a decision.

On every sales call she comes up with a different question and can't make the buying decision now because she has to think about it.

I've tried everything but dynamite to get him to move; he just keeps stalling.

On every sales call she tells me she is going to buy from me but she has to think about it a little while longer.

He seems afraid to make a decision.

The simple fact is that a lot of customers are afraid of making the wrong buying decision. Although most of them will not say that, you will have to deal with it just the same. You will recall that in our earlier discussion of why people do what they do, the important psychological finding was that people do things for which they get rewarded. Another psychological finding is that people don't do things for which they are punished or not rewarded. On that basis, if we look at the mental processes of fear, we discover that fear can be described as "the individual's anticipation of a future negative consequence." In other words, the fearful person thinks that something bad is going to happen to him in the future. This thought is usually connected to an "if–then" relationship: *If* I do this, *then* that will happen. What is interesting about this mental condition of fear is that the negative consequence the person anticipates may never actually exist. In other words, the person is worrying about something that is actually not going to happen. But because the person thinks that it will happen, the fear from the person's point of view is real.

The Four Customer Fears

In analyzing buyers' fears across product lines, we found that all their fears could be categorized in one of the following four ways:

Category 1: They don't understand what you tell them.

Category 2: They don't believe what you tell them.

Category 3: They anticipate possible problems if they buy your product.

Category 4: There really are problems with buying your product.

A customer's fears may stem from one category, from all four categories, or from any combination of them. And since the actions you need to take to deal with one category of fear are not exactly the same as those you need for dealing with another category, your success in handling customer fears is based on your accuracy in categorizing the fears. If you don't address the customer's fears effectively, the customer may not buy at all or may buy from someone else. The selling situation analyses presented in Chapters 15 to 18 will help you identify each category of fear and show you how to deal with it.

15

They Don't Understand What You Tell Them

When customers consider a first-time purchase of hi-tech products, they frequently have difficulty understanding unfamiliar technical jargon and how numerous technical nuances relate to the buying decision.

It is easy to talk about "dumb customers" who repeatedly ask the same questions and "don't understand," but you are the one who loses if you don't get the sale. Because people in general don't want to appear stupid, they frequently indicate that they understand things when in fact they do not. It is not easy for people to say, "Could you please slow down. I am not familiar with the technical terms you are using," or "I am having difficulty understanding how your system (product) works," or "I am confused by the various financing systems you are offering to me." The responses you more probably hear are:

Well, give me some time to digest everything you told me.

You have given me a lot to think about. Why don't you call me next month?

It looks impressive—but we will need some time to decide whether it really is what we need.

These responses may sound positive to you because the customer is planning to think about your product. But if you have established rapport, have correctly identified the customer's needs, and have presented the relevant features and benefits, you have to ask yourself:

1. Why didn't he buy today?
2. What is it that he has to think about?

If the customer has to think about *something*, it must be *something* he does not understand. This happens most frequently under the following conditions:

1. The product is highly technical, and it is made differently or functions quite differently from competitive products.
2. The customer is a first-time buyer of this type of product and is not familiar with the product you are selling.
3. The product involves a high number of choices of facets, options, and add-ons and terms of purchase.
4. Too much information was presented by the salesperson in too short a time period.
5. Information presented by the salesperson was not presented in a logical sequence.
6. The salesperson speaks unintelligibly—mumbles, talks too fast, or uses buzz words and terms unfamiliar to the customer.

The resulting situation is that your customer does not understand what you told him.

Solution

1. Recognize that this situation does not occur because customers are too dumb to understand; it occurs because salespeople are too dumb to explain things so that the customer will understand them. To *manage the buying* in this situation of the customer's lack of understanding, use the following four-step process:

Step 1. Ask questions to find out what specifically the customer does not understand.

Step 2. Give an explanation that the customer will understand.

Step 3. Ask the customer if he or she now understands.

Step 4. Ask the customer to take action.

Steps 2, 3, and 4 are straightforward and present no difficulty. Step 1 is the primary obstacle you must overcome because customers don't volunteer, "This is what I don't understand." Here are some situation examples to help show you how to implement these steps.

Situation Example

CUSTOMER: Well, give me some time to digest everything you told me.

OR

Give me time to think about it.

Step 1. Find out what is not understood.

YOU: You are obviously considering using our service, or you wouldn't be interested in thinking about it. What would be your key concerns at this time?

OR

I appreciate that you are interested in our product. I wonder what it is that you want to think about.

Situation Example

CUSTOMER: It looks impressive, but we will need some time to decide whether it really is what we need.

Step 1. Find out what is not understood.

YOU: I wonder what it is exactly you have to decide.

CUSTOMER: Well, I'm not certain you have exactly what we need.

Step 1. Find out what is not understood.

YOU: I wonder why you say that.

CUSTOMER: Well, your system looks a lot more comprehensive than what we are using now, and it may offer more sophistication than we need at this time.

Step 1. Find out what is not understood.

YOU: What do you mean?

CUSTOMER: Well, we have a small operation here, and we don't want to have to hire a bunch of rocket scientists to operate the equipment.

Step 1. Find out what is not understood.

YOU: Why do you think your people couldn't operate it?

CUSTOMER: Well, it seems that they would be involved in creating their own software, and they are not trained for that.

Step 2. Give explanation.

YOU: I am sorry I gave you the impression that they would be writing software, because they would not. The point I was trying to make was that our system gives your people a lot of flexibility in selecting software to fit their needs, but we supply all the software. I am sorry I wasn't clear on that; your people will not be creating software; they merely have to tell us what they want and we will supply it.

Step 3. Ask if customer understands.

YOU: Does that clear up your concern on that point?
CUSTOMER: Yes, it does.

Step 4. Ask for customer action.

YOU: Do you want to lease the equipment or purchase it?
CUSTOMER: I think we want to go with a 3-year lease.

2. If a customer continues to give evasive answers when you try to uncover a lack of understanding, switch to a more positive approach by reviewing all the reasons why he should buy your product, and then close the sale as follows:

Say to the customer, "You are obviously considering using our service. Before I leave, is there anything we discussed today that you would like me to review with you (or give you more details on)?" If the answer is "no," ask, "If you had to make a decision today whether to buy or not buy our product, what would that decision be?" If he says he would not buy it, ask more questions to find out why. (If he says he would buy it, ask for the customer to take action now.)

OR

Say, "As a check on myself, I wonder if I could take just a few more minutes of your time so I can be sure I didn't leave any important information out. For example, do you agree that (then briefly present each important point of your presentation as it relates to his needs, and ask for his agreement or under-standing)?" Then ask the customer to take action.

3. As mentioned earlier, plan every word of your presentation. Record your presentation and listen to yourself. Make pre-sentations to your friends and relatives and see if they can understand what you are talking about. And practice, prac-tice, practice.

4. Use questions frequently during your presentation to get feedback from the customer that she understands (*a*) what you are saying and (*b*) its importance to her.

   But *don't* ask, "Do you understand?" Ask a question that can be answered only if she understands. Some effective questions are:

   - How important are these technical aspects to you?
   - What kind of importance would you place on this feature?
   - How would you rate these benefits in order of importance to you?
   - What value might this feature be to you?
   - I wonder, how would you describe this in your own words?
   - How might you describe this to your committee?
   - It would help me to know how important this benefit is to you.
   - I went over this quickly (even though you really didn't). I wonder how you would describe it.
   - From your point of view, how would you describe the relationship between _____ and _____ of our service?

  - Do you agree that (the benefits) I have just described will answer the need you mentioned earlier?

5. Use graphic illustrations and audiovisual aids to communicate technical or voluminous or difficult-to-understand information. Draw diagrams; show videos; use handouts of preprinted sketches, schematics, or flowcharts; and be sure to use color or some other method to highlight important statistics appearing on long lists.

6. If this situation frequently occurs because of the complexity of your product, create a written summary of your presentation: At the end of your presentation, together with the customer, list what you want the customer to know and understand. You write the list, but you ask the customer to tell you what to write.

7. If you handle this situation successfully, ask the customer to take action. If you do not handle this situation successfully and the sales call will end, ask the customer to take action.

16

They Don't Believe What You Tell Them

It may shock you to discover that some customers think you are lying to them or at best failing to tell the whole truth. In the real world it is the customer's job to doubt whether or not you are telling the truth, and the more experience customers have in buying things, the more likely they will not trust what salespeople tell them. Their experience can vary from buying an expensive watch at one-third the value to later learn that the mechanism is worth one-tenth what they paid for it, to buying land as an investment which later turns out to be under water.

People have bought boxes of merchandise to discover later that the boxes were empty or short-counted.

People have bought merchandise with a guarantee to later discover that the guarantee is only on paper.

People have bought promised services to later discover that exclusions in the contract's small print make the purchase worthless.

People have bought investments that were promised to preserve capital but that later lose all or most of their capital.

People have bought equipment with promised capacities which can never be achieved.

People have bought things for a specific price to discover later that the real price that must be paid is 10 percent to 100 percent higher.

Perhaps you have had the experience of buying something and not getting what you paid for. You can blame a salesperson for misleading you with lies or unbacked promises or for holding back information about product deficiencies which you didn't ask about. It's also possible that an overly enthusiastic salesperson unintentionally described the product in ambiguous terms, causing confusion or leading you to expect more than could be delivered.

Another issue on rare occasions is that salespeople are tricked by their own company intentionally or through incompetence. The manufacturing department promises delivery dates or product quality which cannot be met; the product research is flawed; or salespeople are lied to by people inside their own company. The net result is that the guiding rule all experienced buyers follow is "Let the buyer beware." In line with this warning, the customer's concerns are:

Is the quality of his product as good as he describes it?

Is she giving me the best price?

Will his product give us the benefits he promises?

Will her company deliver on schedule?

Will his company be in business long enough to fulfill the contract?

Will his company fulfill its obligations under the contract or warranties?

Will her company do what she promises although her promises are not in writing?

Most salespeople do not lie or intentionally mislead customers, and most companies deliver what the customers have paid for. But there are enough exceptions to make buyers wary (afraid). Sometimes customers will not believe you because you are not believable. You may act like you don't know what you are talking about. You may speak without conviction; you interrupt yourself, contradict yourself, seem unsure of what you are talking about, and fumble with your papers when looking for something in your attaché or sample case. If the customers don't think you know what you are talking about, they will anticipate that they will either be talked into buying the wrong thing or not be helped to buy the right thing. Customers in this situation are stalling in making the buying decision because they do not believe what you say about your product or service and your company's ability to deliver. They are afraid they will not get what they will pay for.

You begin to get that sinking feeling in the pit of your stomach that things are not going right when the customer says:

It sounds good in theory, but I'm not sure it will work in our real world.

You keep saying your new line will sell well, but I am the one who has to eat the inventory if it doesn't sell.

We tried something like that a few years ago, and it didn't work for us.

We have heard promises like that before; unfortunately, they didn't work out.

Sometimes you get into the dance of death with the customer with this kind of argument:

CUSTOMER: I think it is too complicated for our people to handle.

SALESPERSON: No it isn't; it's quite simple to operate.

CUSTOMER: Well, it looks too complicated to me.

SALESPERSON: It really isn't; it only looks complicated because you are not familiar with it.

CUSTOMER: Well, I think it is.

SALESPERSON: No it isn't; why don't you try it?

CUSTOMER: I can't waste my people's time on things I know will not work.

SALESPERSON: But you are wrong; it really will work.

The customer stands up and says: "Thanks for your time. We will think about it." What he really means is "Don't let the door hit you in the fanny on the way out—and don't come back because your product is not what we need."

The customer has a need for a product like yours; you know your product will help the customer, but the customer doubts that your product is as good as you say it is. From your point of view, you have done your best to communicate how good your product is, but he does not believe what you are saying.

Solution

1. Recognize that the buyer's trust in you and your company is important to getting the sale. In *managing the buying,* the obligation for establishing that trust is totally yours. The level of trust you need, whether it takes minutes or days to establish, is based primarily on what you do, what you say, and how you say it. The difficulty you face in achieving the buyer's trust is related to how that customer's trust has been violated in the past by other salespeople.

   Make sure you are believable by practicing the things you will say and do in front of the customer until you can perform the show professionally and believably. If you have to find papers or other things in your attaché case or sample case, organize them so the same things are always in the same place, and you can retrieve them without fumbling. Give yourself the blind sample case test. Close your eyes and reach into your sample case for one thing. If you can't find it with your eyes closed, your materials are not organized and you will lose eye contact with the customer while fumbling for things during the sales call. Organize your materials so that you will know exactly where they are and you can pass the blindfold test.

2. It is sad but true that your influence in front of the customer has no value beyond the sound of your voice. No matter how convincing you can be personally one-on-one with the customer, you are still just you—one person. Your word and opinions at best are equally weighted against the customer's word and opinions. You are easily faced with a standoff.

The secret to magnifying the weight of what you say a thousandfold is to use proof to support what you say. When you use proof, your words are supported by the weight of your company's research, the experience of many other satisfied customers, or the testimony of third-party experts. Ideally, the proof is bigger than both you and the buyer. The strategy for using proof of what you say is to remove yourself as the proof. You become the person who delivers the proof. Proof is especially effective when you are trying to convince a person who has a lot more education and experience than you. With proof you don't have to be as smart as or smarter than your customer; it's your company that has to be smarter than your customer. Very effective proof in this situation is product endorsements from individuals who have similar education and experience to this customer.

The most effective alternatives for presenting proof are as follows:

- *Research findings*
- *Third-party comments.* Present articles, videos, quotes, reports of (noted/famous/respected) individuals applauding the success of your product.
- *Third party in person.* Invite the customer to meet in person or by phone respected, believable individuals who will attest to what your product will do.
- *Documentaries.* Provide reports by organizations similar to the target customer's organization, describing their experience and the benefits of using your product.
- *Comparison studies.* Present national and international studies showing advantageous results from using your product versus others.
- *Demonstrations and dramatizations.* Show the product's features and benefits by using the actual product itself or a model or by using video or audio presentations. Have the customer touch, taste, manipulate the product; hit unbreakable things with a hammer; submit unburnable things to fire and heat; subject jamproof things to mindless jamming attempts.

- *Test trials and samples.* Get the customer to use your product in his real world to convince himself that what you say is true (a test drive, a 30-day trial, etc.).

3. When a customer implies or expresses doubts about your five-step message, *manage the buying* by using the following process:

Step 1. Ask questions to find out the customer's specific doubts, concerns, fears.

Step 2. Assure the customer his or her concern is an important one.

Step 3. Answer the customer's concern—use proof.

Step 4. Ask the customer if you have answered his or her concern.

Step 5. Ask the customer to take action.

Situation Example

You are presenting a computer record system to a customer who has no previous experience with computer record systems. Her current record system is hard-copy files. At some point the customer says, "I am not sure a system like that will work for our type of business."

Step 1. Find out specific doubts.

YOU: Why do you say that?

CUSTOMER: Well, our files consist of a lot of legal documents, and we can't do away with those legal documents.

Step 2. Assure customer concern is important.

YOU: That makes sense. We have a lot of customers who have a similar concern about losing documents as well as data. Did I give you the impression that you should destroy your legal documents?

CUSTOMER: No, but you did say the system would eliminate some filing, and we can't ignore our legal filing requirements.

Step 3. Answer the concern.

YOU: I appreciate your concern about lost records. Let me assure you that the system we offer does not replace or destroy legal documents. It merely simplifies and speeds up the availability of the information on those legal documents.

If you have sold your system to a customer with similar needs, use that as your proof.

YOU: As an example, let me show you how another company similar to yours was able to speed up its information handling without jeopardizing its legal documents.

OR

With your permission I would like to arrange a phone call for you to speak to a manager in _____ company, which is similar to your company, and has installed our system.

OR

If I could give you a list of companies in the same business as yours that have installed our systems, would that answer your concern about preserving legal documents? (When she says "yes," show her the list.)

If you have a model system—whether or not you have ever sold one—demonstrate it now to the customer. Your demonstration would be most effective if you could use a few of the customer's files in your demonstration.

Step 4. Ask if concern is answered.

YOU: Now that you know how the system works, do you feel your legal documents would be protected?

OR

Based on what you know now, have I answered your concern about protecting legal documents?

OR

If those companies that handle documents similar to yours are satisfied with our system, do you feel confident your legal documents will be protected?

OR

If you had a system like the one I have just shown you, would your legal documents be protected to your satisfaction?

CUSTOMER: Yes.

Step 5. Ask for customer action.

YOU: When is the earliest date you would like to begin the installation of the new system?

CUSTOMER: The first of next month.

Situation Example

You are trying to get a retailer to add your high-quality product to his inventory because your company's national advertising support will add to his store's volume. At some point in your presentation the customer says, "You say your new line will sell well, but I am the one who has to eat the inventory if it doesn't."

Step 1. Find out specific doubts.

YOU: What do you mean?

> OR

Why do you say that?

> OR

What is your concern?

CUSTOMER: What I mean is what I said. You say the line will increase my business, but how do I know that?

Step 2. Assure customer concern is important.

YOU: I can understand how that would be one of your concerns, and you are not the first one of our customers to ask that same question.

Step 3. Answer the concern.

YOU: If I could show you actual sales figures from other retailers similar in size and volume to your business whose business has increased as I mentioned it would increase, would you have more confidence in the new line's potential for you? (If he says yes, show the sales figures.)

> OR

As a successful businessman, you are the best judge of what benefits your business. I am going to show you other retailers' actual comparative results directly related to the addition of the new line. You can decide for yourself whether the new line will work for you. (Show the comparative results.)

> OR

I have to be honest with you—we would not take back the

inventory, but that is not going to be a problem for you; no one who has taken on the new line has had that problem.

OR

If I may use your phone, I would like you to talk to _____ of _____ company who had the same question _____ months ago before he added the new line. I have his permission for you to ask him whether or not his business has increased. (Dial the number.)

Step 4. Ask if concern is answered.

YOU: Have I answered your concerns (or doubts) about the new line's effects on sales volume?

CUSTOMER: Yes.

Step 5. Ask for customer action.

YOU: Do you want to begin with the new inventory on the 1st or 15th of next month?

CUSTOMER: Let's begin on the 15th.

4. Recognize that it is useless to ask the customer to trust you. To get his trust you must do things that would generate that trust, such as:
   - Show up on time for appointments.
   - Promptly return phone calls you're supposed to return.
   - Do the things you said you were going to do.
   - Answer questions specifically rather than being evasive.
   - Admit that you don't know the answer to a buyer's question, and promise to find out the answer.
   - Keep your promises.
   - Don't promise that your company will do something unless your company has agreed to do it.
   - Don't lie.
   - Don't equivocate.
   - Maintain eye contact.

5. Dress for trust. As the old saying goes, the first impression is the most important, so make a good first impression. Be concerned about your appearance from your customer's point of view. John T. Molloy, in his book *Dress for Success*, reports his studies of how the type of clothes a person wears (style and color) influences other people's impressions of that per-

son. Even more important, that impression influences how a person is treated. In other words, the attention, courtesy, cooperation, and trust you want from the people you meet will vary according to the impressions you create by how you dress. As strange as it may seem to you, the impression strangers have about your affluence will vary according to whether they see you wearing a beige or black raincoat.

Also, there are special situations wherein customers in workshirts may not trust salespeople in suits or customers in suits may not trust salespeople in workshirts. Find out your customer's point of view and create the personal appearance that will work for you.

6. When the majority of your customers express the same doubts about your product or service for which you have a good answer, don't wait until the customer mentions his or her doubts to present your answer and proof. You can say, "Some customers have questions about ____ (or "have concerns about," or "think it is important that," or "wonder if"). Is that important to you?"

   The real excitement in presenting a product is to romanticize its strong points by weaving the proof throughout your sales presentation. This influences the customer's opinions in stages (by seconds, minutes, or hours). For example, let's say the product you are trying to sell is structurally stronger than the competition; therefore, multiple units of your product can be stacked higher than any competitor. This could save space for the customer. You know that previous customers doubted the stackability of your product even though you showed them pictures of stacked units. To make your point, you could:

   > Bring multiple units and stack them in front of the customer as you speak.
   >
   > OR
   >
   > Slowly unpack a unit and stand on it while you make your presentation.
   >
   > OR
   >
   > Ask the customer to stand on (or jump up and down on) one of your units.

Whenever possible, get the customer involved in proving to himself what you say is true.

7. It is essential that you don't belittle what the customer thinks is important. Frequently a customer's concern is one you have already heard from several other customers, but the customer believes his concern is important and unique. When you have identified the customer's concern, fear, doubts, assure him that what he is thinking is important but not unusual. Psychologists do that with patients who are upset over their actions or the actions of others which they feel are unique and abnormal. A lot of stress is eliminated when the psychologist assures patients that what they have done or felt has been experienced by others and is normal and perhaps appropriate. An appropriate response to your customer would be:

That's certainly a logical concern for people in your business.

OR

I can understand how that point is important to you in these hard times.

OR

That's certainly a valid question in view of the legal ramifications.

OR

That is a question we hear frequently from our customers in businesses similar to yours.

8. Use the features of your product as proof for delivery of benefits. For example, because the cabinet of your equipment is made out of 10-gauge steel (the feature), it is not damaged when you stack several units on top of each other and less space is required (the benefit). You are explaining to the customer, "Because our product has this (feature), you, therefore, receive this (benefit)." The word *because* is a nice convincing word to use to connect features and benefits. For example:

- Because our service unit is on 24-hour call, we are able to respond immediately to your service needs, eliminating unnecessary equipment downtime for you.

- Because our company invested $2 million to install the latest refining process, the product you receive contains less impurities, which will lower your rejects.
- Because our national advertising produces product demand, you will have increased product turnover per year, and therefore get a greater return on your investment.
- Because our medication gets into the bloodstream quicker, the patient's temperature will drop sooner.

9. Whether you succeed or fail in handling the customer's doubts or concerns, ask the customer to take action.

17

They Anticipate Possible Problems If They Buy Your Product

In this situation the customer understands what you say about your product, believes what you say, and believes your product will satisfy his needs, but he thinks there may be a future negative consequence if he buys your product. Some anticipated problems are tangible, and some are intangible; some could be real possibilities, and some are only imagined. When I ask customers to describe their so-called experience of "fear of buying," this is what they tell me:

I'm worried about making the wrong buying decision.

I'd feel like a fool if I paid more than I had to pay.

If this doesn't work, I could lose my job.

My career in this company is resting on this deal.

This purchase is making a long-term commitment; I want to be sure it's the right one.

Because my business is small, the wrong decision could put me out of business.

I worked a long time to save this money; it's all I have, and I don't want to make the wrong investment and lose it if Congress changes the tax laws.

These comments obviously reflect a personal concern. The buyer in each instance anticipates that if he makes the wrong buying decision, he will be harmed personally in some way. In many organizations, people who make bad buying decisions don't get promoted, can get demoted, or can even lose their job. But these fears can also be product-related, as evident in the following comments:

With the rapid changes in technology these days, it's tough to decide whether to buy now or wait a year to see how much the technology improves.

This supplier has not been around too long; if I commit to their system and they go belly up, I will be left high and dry without a supplier.

If we make this purchase and the economy slips into a recession, we could end up with a debt problem.

With the current changes in the laws, only God knows what our liability might be a year from today if we switch to this new material.

These customers have real concerns about what will happen in their world if they buy your product. But if they don't express their fear, you cannot deal with it. What is most unfortunate is that sometimes they do express their fear, but the salesperson ignores it or treats it in an offhanded manner. When somebody is concerned about something, the correct answer is not, "Don't worry about it."

Please note that this is not a customer who thinks you are lying about your product. He merely believes there are other conditions that may or may not be within your control that will be detrimental if this purchase is made. Sometimes concerns about future problems connected with the purchase are triggered by rumors about your product and company, such as:

I hear they're having labor problems over there.

I heard there's a management shake-up going on.

I hear they have financial problems; if they go into Chapter 11, what do we do for our supplies?

I hear their new product is going to be recalled because there are some questions about its safety.

I hear they are going to reduce their dealer network, which could mean that instead of having a local person to deal with, we will end up talking to an answering machine 500 miles away.

This kind of information could be true or just rumors or neither. It could be relevant or irrelevant to your company's ability to deliver a quality product or service at a reasonable price. But if the customer believes the information is true, you are faced with an obstacle to getting the sale. The customer anticipates future problems if he buys your product.

Sometimes you will call on past customers of your company who don't buy from you now because of how badly your company treated them in the past. Whether that bad treatment was by accident or by intent is not relevant; the customer was treated badly and rightfully expects that it could happen again. This is rarely a mystery, because they will tell you:

I wouldn't buy from your company if it was the last one on earth.

All of you guys are a bunch of thieves. Get out of here and stop bothering me.

Tell your boss to drop dead, and if you come around here again, I'll have you arrested for trespassing.

Obviously, all these customers intend to avoid the anticipated problems of dealing with your company.

Solution

1. By now, you should have gotten the message that information is the basis for successful *managing the buying*—information you collect from your customer, information the customer collects from you. You have to find out

what the customer is thinking before you can provide the correct response. Fortunately, customers in this situation will usually tell you what problems they anticipate, and you can use the following five-step process to deal with it.

Step 1. Ask questions to find out the customer's specific doubts, concerns, fears.

Step 2. Assure the customer his or her concern is an important one.

Step 3. Answer the customer's concern—use proof.

Step 4. Ask the customer if you have answered his or her concern.

Step 5. Ask the customer to take action.

Situation Example

There is a management shake-up in your organization, but it has no effect on how you deliver your product. The customer said, "I read in the newspaper that there are going to be a lot of management changes at your company."

Step 1. Find out the customer's concern.

YOU: Is that a concern for you?

CUSTOMER: Certainly. If you go through some big shake-up, how can I know you will continue to supply me.

Step 2. Assure concern is important.

YOU: A lot of customers have asked me questions about that.

Step 3. Answer the concern.

YOU: I've checked into that. My manager has assured me that these changes are at the executive level and really have no impact on how we produce our product and service our customers, and since this business is so successful, we plan to be around for a long time.

Step 4. Ask if concern is satisfied.

YOU: Does that answer your concern?

CUSTOMER: Yes.

Step 5. Ask the customer to take action.

YOU: Will I be able to get a purchase order today?

CUSTOMER: If you don't mind waiting, I will have my secretary type it up.

Situation Example

The customer has just said, "I heard that your organization may be filing for bankruptcy."

Step 1. Find out the customer's concern.

YOU: How is that important to you?

CUSTOMER: Well, if you folks go out of business, I will have to find a new supplier.

Step 2. Assure concern is important.

YOU: I am just as concerned as you are about this because this company pays my salary, and so I've checked with my manager about this.

Step 3. Answer the concern.

YOU: What she has told me is that filing for bankruptcy is a legal procedure to support a reorganization plan and that the company has full intention of continuing in this business. So you can bet on seeing me around here for a long time in the future.

Step 4. Ask if concern is satisfied.

YOU: Does that clear up your concern?

CUSTOMER: Yes.

Step 5. Ask the customer to take action.

YOU: Will this be a cash transaction, or will you want to use our finance service?

CUSTOMER: What rate of interest can I get from your finance service?

2. When the customer has not verbalized the problems he anticipates and is stalling long beyond the point where you

think the sale should have been made, it would be reasonable to say, "I've been calling on you for (specify number of days, weeks, months) now and we've talked a lot about your needs and what our product can do for you, and yet it appears that you are still uncertain. (Step 1) What concerns do you have that appear to be preventing you from making this decision?"

Or you could say, "I would like to take the time today to sum up what we have talked about over the last (specify period of time)." Then list the customer's needs as he specified them. Next list the features and benefits of your product that will satisfy those needs. Then say, (step 1) "Is there anything we have left out here that is of concern to you?" and wait for the customer's answer. If the customer answers "yes," ask him what they are and answer them. If the answer is "no," (step 5) ask the customer to take action.

If you've spent a lot of time with a customer, it would certainly be appropriate to say, (step 1) "We have spent a lot of time together, could you please tell me why you're not buying my product?" Or you could say, "There seems to be something bothering you about this situation. Would you like to share it with me?" Or you could use the killer of all questions, "What do I have to do to get you to buy my product?"

If you are successful in using your questioning technique, you will discover that customers don't stall without reason. You may not yet know the reason, but they have one.

3. When dealing with a customer's concern, it is helpful to say that other customers have had the same concern. This tends to make the customer's questions appear less unusual and reduces some tension. You say, for example,

(Step 2) "Yes, a lot of customers in the past have expressed that same concern about our ability to make truck deliveries in the winter time when the heavy snows arrive. (Step 3) But happily for us, we haven't missed deliveries as have our competitors because we have more distribution centers and our trucks travel a shorter distance to service you."

4. If a customer is not buying because she imagines future problems related to possible but not probable technology developments, changes in laws, or unpredictable economic conditions, it is difficult for you to deal with. Since no one is able to predict the future, much less what lawmakers will do, your claim that these things will most likely not occur do not share equal weight with the customer's prediction that they will occur. It is always possible that the customer's predictions about an unpleasant future are based on erroneous information. If this is true, you can arm yourself with more exact information and draw a more convincing picture for the customer that the unpleasant future she expects is less likely to occur.

   However, if this alternative is not available, the logical solution is to create a scenario that convinces the customer that the actual losses in delaying the buying decision are far greater than making the buying decision now. The emphasis has to be on how much the customer will gain over the near term because she made this purchase versus how much she will lose over the long term because of this purchase.

   It also helps to show the buyer alternatives for avoiding or getting out of some imagined future undesirable position. There are always possibilities for trade-ins, contract buyouts, and other methods of cutting losses if the imagined nasty future event actually arrives.

5. It may be hard to believe, but the easiest customer to deal with in these situations is the one who is afraid of losing his or her job because of the buying decision. But this is only easy to deal with if you uncover all the aspects of the individual's fear. When you become fully informed, you will discover that the apprehensions are usually related to anticipated product failure. When you identify that as a problem, your solutions are the same as in the first category, which is, "They don't believe what you're telling them."

6. There are occasions when the fear (anticipated problem) surrounding the purchase involves the individual's career because the buyer would be instituting a new system, new process, or some change that may alienate other people in

the organization. Your solution in this instance is to get the other people involved in the buying decision. By sharing the responsibility for the buying decision, you get the buyer off the hook.

7. If the problem is that the customer was treated badly as a result of how you make your product, service it, deliver it, or require payment for it, and those conditions have not changed, you should go someplace else for your business.

8. If this customer is carrying a grudge because your company treated him badly in the past, you may never solve this problem. But if this customer's buying power is important to you, here are some things you can do.

   a. Find out exactly what your company did to this customer. You can ask the customer if he will talk to you. Your initial approach is to separate yourself in the customer's eyes from the company or whoever it was that treated him badly. It is easy to explain that you are different from the person he dealt with in the past. You are trying to make a living as a salesperson, and you would like to meet with him to deliver an apology for how he has been treated in the past. The initial objective is to open communications rather than sell your product. If the customer will not talk to you, you can try talking to his staff.

   b. If the customer was treated poorly by accident or through a misunderstanding, or if someone who is no longer with your company treated the customer badly, you have a chance to correct the situation. Your strategy is quite simple:

      ▪ Let the customer know you are aware of the problem.

      ▪ Convince the customer that the situation has changed, and if necessary, get higher-level people in your organization to apologize and promise better treatment.

   c. Beg for the business or some portion of the business as a test of your company's sincerity. When all else fails, begging is a reasonable alternative. "I need your business. What do I have to do to get it?" or "Please give me a chance with a small order, and if we don't treat you right, I will never bother you again." You can also use promises like, "If you will give me some of your business, I promise to take special care of you" (or "I promise to give you special attention"). If this customer is important to your company, you may also be able to get promises from higher-level individuals in your organization verbally or in writing that you will do everything in your power not to treat this customer as badly as your company has in the past.

9. In step 4, after answering a customer concern, you should always ask, "Does this answer your concern?" If the answer is "no," ask "Why?" or "What else do you have on your mind?" or "What else are you thinking about?" or "What else are you concerned about?" If the answer is "yes," ask for the customer to take action that will advance the sale.

18

There Really Are Problems with Buying Your Product

As the saying goes, "It's not a perfect world, and nobody has the perfect product to sell." If you think you are the exception by having the perfect product, you will discover that your perfect product is not perfect for all your customers. So like the rest of us, you will face customers' refusals to buy your perfect product because, from the customers' point of view, they will be harmed in some way by the purchase.

What's really nice about this situation is that the customers' concerns are generally not hidden. Customers will usually tell you in no uncertain terms:

Your price is too high.

We don't want to buy. We're only looking for a lease. (You don't have a lease.)

Your product doesn't meet all our specifications.

If we change to your system, we are going to have to retrain everyone, and we can't afford that cost right now.

Your unit takes up too much space.

I agree your product is good, but the order quantities you require are too high; we would have no place to store the materials.

Your machine takes too long to warm up.

All our supplies fit the old system. If I buy your system, I'm going to have to eat the cost for those supplies we can't use; we can't afford to do that.

Yes, you have a good product, but the cost is almost twice as much as we planned to spend, so it looks like we can't afford it.

Your product shelf life is too short.

Your package is too difficult to open.

Our customers don't buy that kind of ethnic product.

Your product is too upscale for us, and if we put it on the shelf, it will be stolen.

Frequently customers will even admit that they would like to own your product but will not do so because of the reasons they state.

You usually get this customer confrontation immediately after you ask him to buy your product. The sales presentation has rolled along with great style, wit, and professionalism; the customer has shown a lot of interest, but when you ask for the order, the customer says, "No sale." Most salespeople dread this confrontation so much they actually avoid asking the customer to buy. Many salespeople tell me that before making a sales call, they pray to their favorite deity, asking, "Please don't let him tell me my price is too high"; or "Please don't let him notice our high minimum ordering quantity"; or "Please don't let him bring up that training problem"; or "Please don't let him notice how difficult it is to open our package."

But, unfortunately, customers notice these things, and so the salesperson packs up his bag and leaves muttering to himself. The only solutions seem to be to sell to dumber customers or have the company make the product more perfect. Experienced salespeople know that in selling you don't get every sale, but many of them are losing too many sales because they are not dealing successfully with the customer's concerns about the problems associated with the purchase. These concerns about problems with buying your product exist because either:

> Your product satisfies most but not all of your customer's needs

OR

> Your product satisfies your customer's needs but actually creates a problem or discomfort if the purchase is made.

When we compare all salespeople across all product lines who know their product, who get to know their customer, and who work a full day, we find large numbers of them are not as successful as they could be because they are unable to satisfy or eliminate customers' real concerns about the product. When these concerns are not satisfied, you will lose sales.

We are talking about a customer who has a need for your product, has expressed interest in your product, and has agreed with you that the benefits your product can provide are solutions to his or her needs. You have asked for the the order, and the customer responds with concerns about some negative aspects of the purchase which appear to be obstacles to getting the sale.

Solution

1. The good news is that the concern the customer has expressed is usually the only reason why he will not buy your product. If you can satisfy or eliminate that concern, you will have *managed the buying* and will get the sale. Even more good news is that most customer concerns can be satisfied or eliminated. Notice the difference between the term *satisfied* and the term *eliminated. Eliminated* clearly means you or your company has removed or taken away something negative. *Satisfied* means that you have given the customer reasons to overlook what he thought was a negative aspect of your product.

   Don't dread these situations, thinking "I hope he does not notice...." Approach them with the positive expectation, "If I handle this customer's concern, I will get the sale."

2. Accept the fact that your product is not perfect for every customer, and so don't try to hide the defects of your product, especially if you're looking for repeat business.

3. Dealing with a customer who just gave you a reason for not buying your product is one of those critical "moments of truth" when your success or failure depends on what you say next. Too much is riding on it for you to leave it to chance.

   Make up a list of the concerns your customers have expressed in the past about the defects of your product, service, or ability to deliver. If you've never sold before, your sales manager could probably give you such a list. Then make up a list of the most effective answers that deal with each concern. For example, if you sell the highest-priced product and customers frequently state "high price" as their reason for not buying, you have to have an answer or a solution for that concern. You have to give the customer a reason to pay the higher price.

   When I consult with companies to improve their sales performance, I get them to collect from all their salespeople all the reasons customers give for not buying their products. I then get them to collect the best answers each salesperson has developed to deal with each reason. Most sales groups initially resist this effort because it seems like an endless project. As one sales representative said, "It will look like the *Yellow Pages*." But interestingly, there is a finite list of concerns customers have about a specific product. The list only changes if the competition changes its products or terms of sale. Once the lists are completed, the most effective answers are selected and all the salespeople are trained in how to give the most effective answer for each reason. Salespeople are no longer surprised when customers state their concern for negative aspects of the sale; they are prepared to respond effectively to every customer concern, and, as a result, sales increase.

   Once you pick the correct method of answering each concern, write down your answer word for word and practice, practice, and practice again so you will say it flawlessly.

4. Besides knowing the correct answers, it is critical that you choose the correct answer for each situation. Your basis for doing that is correctly understanding what the customer has just said to you. For example, if one customer says to you, "The price is high," and another customer says, "The price is too high," they are not saying the same thing. For example, the first customer may mean:

The price is more than I expected to pay.

OR

It's more expensive than the one I currently own.

OR

It's more expensive than the last one I bought.

OR

It's more expensive than most similar products on the market.

OR

It's as expensive as I thought it was going to be.

Whereas the second customer may mean:

The manufacturer is charging too much for the product.

OR

I can't afford to pay that much.

OR

The price you want me to pay is not worth the value I expect to get out of owning your product.

OR

I can get the same value from your competition at a lower price.

OR

I can't afford to pay that much for your product.

OR

If I give the salesperson some resistance, he might give me a discount.

If you respond to both of these customers in the same way, you may be creating more problems than you already have, because both customers are not giving you a reason for not buying your product. The first customer may be merely commenting on the state of things. It is the second customer who appears to be giving you a reason for not buying your product. If you in fact do have the highest-priced product on the market, it doesn't mean that every customer's comments about price is an obstacle to your getting a sale. For example, if a customer asks you, "How much is your product?" or "Is your product high priced?" or "How does it compare in price?" she is really expressing an interest in owning your product; otherwise she wouldn't be thinking about price. In selling parlance this is called a *buying signal*; that is, the customer is giving you a signal that she's interested in owning your product.

Recently when I was traveling with a salesperson selling a skin care product, he told me a story about a customer who irritated him. He said he had made a sales presentation to this customer emphasizing that although his product had a name similar to other skin care products, it was actually quite different and should be considered in a separate category. "But this dumb customer never got the point," he said. "When I finished explaining how different my product was from the other products, he asked me how my product compared in price to those products." When I asked the salesperson why that bothered him, he said, "The customer knew my product was high-priced, and he was just trying to give me a hard time." He became silent for quite awhile after I explained to him that when a customer asks about price, he is expressing an interest in owning the product; it is a buying signal. That customer was not trying to give him a hard time; he was expressing an interest in owning the product.

Before deciding which answer to give, classify the customer's comment into one of the two following categories:

a. The customer comment is merely a statement of fact.

b. The customer is stating his reason not to buy.

5. *If you interpret a customer's comment as a statement of fact,* you have the following alternative responses.

   a. The best approach is to remain silent after the customer comments. But look at the customer expectantly as though he is going to continue speaking. Frequently, if you allow time for the customer to speak, he continues to talk beyond his previous comment, he gives more information, and frequently the sale progresses. If the customer does not resume talking after the silence, ask the customer to take action. It can be the same action question that prompted the initial customer statement, or it can be a different action question which will also advance the sale. Don't worry about asking a different action question. Once you get the sale progressing again, you can always return to the question that was not answered.

b. As another approach, if the customer does not respond after your silence, you could ask, "Is that a problem for you?" and wait for the response. You ask this latter question to find out whether the customer's comment is merely a statement of fact or whether he is giving you a reason not to buy.

Situation Example

Customer is buying a luxury car.

YOU: You said you like the sporty looks of the two-door model but you could use the extra space of the four-door model? Which one do you think would fit most of your needs?

CUSTOMER: What is your best price on that four-door model?

YOU: $52,000 plus tax.

CUSTOMER: Wow! That's a high-priced automobile!

YOU: (After a few moments of silence) Do you want to finance that through your own bank or use our commercial financing plan?

CUSTOMER: I'll run it through my own bank.

Situation Example

Same customer as above.

CUSTOMER: Wow! That's a high-priced automobile!

YOU: (After a few moments of silence) Is that a problem for you?

CUSTOMER: No, it is just more money than I ever paid for a car.

YOU: Do you want to finance that through your bank or use our commercial financing plan?

CUSTOMER: I'll run it through my bank.

Situation Example

Customer is buying a new business system.

YOU: To summarize, you've agreed with me that our system will not only speed up information processing for you but also improve your capacity to computerize your inventory, which you're not able to do on your current system. When would you like to have our system operating for you?

CUSTOMER: If we go with your system, we're going to have to train everybody on this new system.

YOU: (After a few moments of silence) Would it be most convenient for us to come here and train your people, or would you like to send them to our branch office in small groups?

CUSTOMER: It would give us more flexibility if you could come here to train our people.

Situation Example

You are selling a shredder to an executive in an office with antique decor.

YOU: Based on the information you have given me, you could use one medium-size unit to handle your volume of documents, or you could use two small units, one for you and one for your secretary. What do you think would be best for you?

CUSTOMER: I would like to have one for my own use, as well as one for my secretary, but, gosh, that's an awfully ugly unit. I'd hate to have it in my beautiful office.

YOU: (After a few moments of silence) Where will you put it?

CUSTOMER: I can put it in next to the credenza and hide it behind a potted plant.

Situation Example

Your customer is a retail-store owner selling home decorating supplies. Your product is a new line of coordinated items so that chair coverings, wall coverings, tablecloths, etc., can be matched and coordinated. In addition to improved service to customers, it increases dollars sales per customer.

YOU: Based on everything you've seen today, would you rather start off with plan 1 or plan 2?

CUSTOMER: I don't know. This business has been in a slump for the last 8 months; no one knows how bad it's going to get.

YOU: (After a few moments of silence) Would plan 1 or plan 2 be best to serve your current customer profile?

CUSTOMER: I think plan 1 would be best to start with. We can always upgrade to plan 2 later.

6. *If you interpret a customer's comment as a reason not to buy,* you have to eliminate or satisfy that concern to get the sale. You know for certain you are in this situation when the customer actually tells you she is not going to buy your product. For example,

> Thanks for your time, but I can get it for 15 percent less from your competitor.
>
> We can't wait 3 months for delivery. Your competitor is going to deliver within 10 days.
>
> Your product is interesting, but because of the economic slowdown, we are not buying anything right now.
>
> Buying your product will require an additional investment in training, and we have decided to stick with the old system.

   a. For you to deal successfully with this category of customer response, it is crucial that you do not decide that the sale is lost (today) until you are out on the street. If you decide during the sales call that the customer is not going to buy, you will give up trying to deal effectively with the customer's concerns. *Your underlying assumption throughout all your selling activities must be that the customer is going to buy your product if you do the right things.*

   When the customer states his negative concern, it sounds to you like he's saying, "I'm not going to buy your product because I can get it cheaper from your competitor." If you make that conclusion, the sales call is over and you have lost a sale. But if you conclude that he means only that he is *not yet* going to buy your product, the sale will continue. He will buy your product if you satisfy his concern or eliminate it as an obstacle to buying.

As we know, people do not always buy the lowest-priced products or services, and they do buy products in spite of their concerns about some negative aspects of the purchase. They obviously have reasons for doing that. The customer who tells you that she is not going to buy your product because the competitor's price is lower is really telling you, "You haven't given me any reasons why I should pay the higher price for your product." This customer would have made it easier for you by saying, "Why should I pay more money for your product when I can get it from your competition 15 percent cheaper?" You would not consider the sale lost, and you would continue the selling process trying to answer the customer's question. One key to dealing successfully with customers' concerns about the negative aspects of your product is to assume that no matter how she states her concern, she is really asking you, "Why should I buy your product when...?"

Your answers will fall into one of the following two categories:

(1) You will show your customer ways around this negative aspect of the purchase, thereby eliminating it.

OR

(2) You will emphasize the value gained from the purchase, which outweighs the negative aspect of the purchase (which cannot be removed), thereby satisfying the customer's concern.

b. The answers under category (1) are usually solutions to the customer's concern. Sometimes these solutions are provided by your company, but mostly they are the result of your own creativity. For example, one salesperson was having difficulty selling his product to small manufacturers because the minimum-order quantity by a single customer would be over a year's supply for that one customer and would tie up a lot of capital in inventory. The salesperson's solution was to create a cooperative buying arrangement among four small manufacturing companies only for the purpose of ordering this product. The salesperson made the sale, and the customers received the product in smaller, usable quantities.

There are salespeople who have found secondary markets for the customer's inventory of competitive materials that become unusable because of the new product purchased. If the customer could not have disposed of the inventory, the sale would not have been made.

One salesperson, faced with losing a sale because his product did not meet the customer's specifications, conducted a detailed analysis of the specifications with the customer's engineering department and discovered the specifications were outdated. The engineering department agreed that two of the specifications that the salesperson's product did not meet were too high and could be lowered. He got the sale.

Salespeople selling large-size business equipment to small businesses with limited space often have to do space-use analysis for the customer in order to get the sale.

Solutions provided by your company are usually beyond what you could do on your own. For example, customers who cannot purchase because of limited cash may receive extended payment terms. Financial institutions having difficulty selling lower-rated bonds have provided insurance to guarantee payments in order to overcome the customer's concern. Customers claiming lack of inventory space receive personal inventory management analysis by the sales representative, frequently demonstrating to the customer that some inventory being carried is unproductive. Whatever the solution is, it must really satisfy the customer's concern about that problem.

How you describe the solution is not critical as long as your customer understands it and believes you. If you explain your solution too fast or in a confusing or incomplete way, you will lose the sale, so don't rush it.

c. The negative aspect in category (2) cannot be made to disappear; it can only be shown to be of less importance as a negative aspect than the value gained from making the purchase. A basic understanding of human behavior leads us to conclude that the value or pleasure of doing something in life must be greater than the pain a person must go through to be able to do that thing. This is the pivotal point for your strategy in dealing with the customer who has decided that the pain of owning your product is greater than the pleasure of owning your product. When you cannot remove that pain, you must show a benefit for buying which is greater than the pain.

For the customer who says, "I don't have shelf space in my store for another breakfast cereal," the answer is to demonstrate how your company's national advertising creates higher product turnover, which will bring in more income for the same shelf space over a specified period. Therefore, the buyer's choice is, "Which of the slow movers should be replaced by this potential high-moving product?"

A customer's concern about the added cost of operator training if he buys your system must be balanced by some significant benefit of owning your system, such as increased speed, reliability, added capacity, accuracy, eventual ease of operation, manpower savings, etc.

The customer concerned about paying 15 percent more for your product has to be shown the value of that choice. And the value of that choice must be based on product differentiation—the differences in benefits to the customer because of differences in the products (delivery, service, reliability, etc.). The customer must get something for the additional cost in buying your product that would not be received if the competitive product were purchased. Your higher-priced product may function with less downtime, lower maintenance costs, and higher accuracy, which in the long run could be shown to be a total lower cost. If your product really performs better over time, the most convincing arguments avoid the comparison of purchase price but emphasize the total cost-benefit over long periods of time. A car battery that truly lasts forever could be fairly high priced but still be cheaper in the long run than a less expensive car battery that must be changed every 3 years.

When talking about product differentiation, do not exclude the intangible benefits the customer can derive, such as pride of ownership, object of envy, maintaining his or her reputation, expression of love, safety, etc. For example, there are men who will pay 300 percent of the list price of a new sports car to be the first in town to drive one. There are women who will pay $3000 for a dress to wear for a special occasion and never wear it a second time.

7. I have observed salespeople who agreed with the customer when a negative fact was stated:

    CUSTOMER: $52,000 is a lot of money for a car.
    SALESPERSON: Yes, you're right; do you want the two-door or the four-door?

    I have seen this response work in some selling situations. But I would rather not do that. Although there are negative aspects of my product and the customer knows that, I'd rather not agree with the customer. This doesn't mean I'm hiding those negatives aspects. It just means I don't want to do anything to push the customer in a negative direction. If our product is ugly and I know that it's ugly and the customer knows it's ugly, that's fine. But I will not offer to agree with the customer that it's ugly. That does not advance the sale. If the customer said to me, "Don't you think it's ugly?" I might say, "I've heard some people say that. Where are you going to put it?"

8. As you may conclude by now, customers have a lot of concerns when they are involved in purchasing a product or service. There are some sales training philosophies that will tell you that you must deal with all these concerns before you can get the sale. That is not true. There are car buyers who are concerned about the low gas mileage of a luxury automobile, but they buy it and even pay the gas guzzler tax. There are people who are concerned about the amount of work required for maintaining a swimming pool but buy the swimming pool anyhow. There are people who are concerned about the raw danger of operating chain saws but

buy one to cut their firewood. You might also say that one of the major concerns of customers is that they have to spend their money to acquire your product or service, but for the most part, that is not an obstacle to making the sale.

9. When responding to the customer comment that you interpret as *a reason not to buy,* use the right words in the right order. The recommended six-step process to *manage the buying* in this situation is as follows:

Step 1. Ask questions to find out the customer's specific concern.

Step 2. Make sure that this is a concern that is an obstacle to the sale. If the customer has not actually told you he will not buy your product, ask, "Is that a problem for you?"

Step 3. When a customer clarifies for you that it is a problem and a reason to not buy your product, find out if this is the only reason blocking the sale by asking, "Is there any other reason why you would not buy my product?" or "If I could solve this problem for you, would you then buy my product?" If the customer says other concerns are blocking the sale, ask what they are and repeat steps 1 and 2.

Step 4. If there is no other reason blocking the sale, answer the customer's concern.

Step 5. When you finish answering the customer's concern(s), find out if you have succeeded by asking, "Does that satisfy your concern?" If the answer is "yes," go to step 6. If the answer is "no," repeat steps 1 through 4.

Step 6. Ask the customer to take action.

Situation Example

You are selling a plain-paper desktop fax machine to the administrative partner of a small law firm employing eight lawyers. You have just mentioned the price of your unit.

CUSTOMER: Thanks for your time, but XYZ company is more price competitive.

Step 1. Find out the customer's specific concern.

YOU: What do you mean by that?

CUSTOMER: I can buy the same unit from your competitor for 15 percent less. (The customer doesn't mean the *same* unit, because your company is the only one selling this machine. The customer means another desktop fax machine by another company.)

Step 2. Find out if it is an obstacle to the sale.

YOU: Is that a problem for you?

CUSTOMER: It is not a problem for me because I am going to save $240.

YOU: Which model fax machine are you talking about?

CUSTOMER: I'm talking about the X-53 made by _____.

Step 3. Is this the only reason?

YOU: If there was no difference in price, which machine would you buy?

CUSTOMER: I'd buy yours.

Step 4. Answer the concern.

YOU: I'm glad to hear that. A lot of our customers feel the same way. I'd like to do some cost comparisons for you to demonstrate that it will actually cost you more in the long run to buy their machine than our machine. For example, the reason why they have discounted their machine is because it is a roll-fed coated-paper machine. We previously sold coated-paper machines, but our company designed machines that handle plain paper for several reasons. One reason is that the coated paper, although it makes good copies, is a very thin paper that frequently gives finger cuts to the people who handle the copies. Secondly, you have to buy the roll paper from their company, which means that you don't have flexibility of suppliers. With us you have flexibility because you can use any plain paper which you can buy in very large quantities from the supplier of your choice and, therefore, get at a low price.

Another problem you have with coated paper is that it curls up and is difficult to file; not only that, but the image fades over time. That's why people who have coated-paper faxes recopy the faxes they receive onto plain paper. This means not only are you paying for the copy of the fax on the coated paper, but you are also paying the additional costs of time and paper for having it copied on your copy machine. You don't have to do that with our machine.

Based on the number of copies you told me you produce per day, I have worked up a little analysis here to compare costs for both machines over the year. (This concern is mentioned frequently, and so you previously worked up a cost analysis to fit various copy-use levels so you would have the answer when you needed it.) You can see here (show example) that in the first 6 months of using the competitive machine, your higher costs of operation will equal the $240 you thought you saved on the purchase. And in the following 6 months you'll lose twice that amount.

Step 5. Ask if concern is answered.

YOU: Do you see that in the long run you will save more money by buying our machine?

CUSTOMER: Yes, I wasn't aware of the difference between the plain- and coated-paper machines.

Step 6. Ask for customer action.

YOU: Which day next week is a good day to deliver your machine?

CUSTOMER: How about Wednesday morning?

Situation Example

You are selling a coated-paper desktop fax machine to the administrative partner of a small law firm and you haven't yet mentioned the price of your unit.

CUSTOMER: I don't think your machine is right for us.

Step 1. Find out the customer's specific concern.

YOU: I wonder why.

CUSTOMER: Well, your machine prints on coated paper.

Step 2. Find out if it is an obstacle to the sale.

YOU: Is that a problem for you?

CUSTOMER: Yes, we don't want a coated-paper machine.

YOU: I wonder why.

CUSTOMER: Well, we went through that with copiers years ago, and we feel that the copies on plain paper are more suited to the image we want to project to our clients.

Step 3. Is this the only reason?

YOU: I've heard that comment occasionally from legal firms. I can understand why image is very important to your business. Is there any other reason why you would not buy my machine?

CUSTOMER: No.

Step 4. Answer the concern.

YOU: Can I ask you a few questions? Some of my friends in your same business have told me that business has been slowing steadily for the last 2 years. Would you say the economy has had an effect on your business also?

CUSTOMER: Well, people always need legal advice, but our business has slowed down a little bit lately; there has been a drop-off in the commercial end of the business.

YOU: The other firms in that situation are also concerned about controlling operating costs. Is that a similar concern of yours?

CUSTOMER: Yes, in these times we always look to eliminate unnecessary costs wherever we can.

YOU: I am glad to hear you are interested in cutting costs because there are several advantages to using the coated paper that you will not get with your plain-paper machines. First of all, the coated-paper machine is roll-fed, and because the paper is so thin, we are able to get the equivalent of more $8\frac{1}{2}$ inch by 11 inch sheets on a roll than you get in the typical cassette of a plain-paper machine. The benefit to you is that your staff spends less time servicing the machine to add paper. Another interesting feature that you can only have with the roll-fed machine is that it only uses a full sheet when a full sheet is necessary. For example, when someone faxes you an invoice or message on paper that is less than the normal 11-inch length, our machine will cut the paper to match the size needed. With the sheet-fed plain-paper machine a full sheet of paper is used whether or not it is needed.

Since experience has shown that approximately 10 percent of all fax messages are on shorter pieces of paper, you get the equivalent of 10 percent more paper use on our roll than you can out of your plain-paper cassette. Another advantage of our machine is that you can receive legal-size messages without changing the paper. To put that ability on a plain-paper machine, you will have to buy the larger unit with two paper cassettes, and that will cost an additional $500. Would the savings in paper costs contribute to your current cost-control plans?

CUSTOMER: Yes.

YOU: Another important difference, which a lot of people don't know about until they are faced with the problem, is jamming. Jamming occurs when a piece of paper is fed into the machine for a copy but it gets stuck in the process. This jamming process only occurs when the new edge of paper is entering the roller-feed mechanism. However, with our roll-fed machines, there is only one edge that enters the rollers for the several hundred copies that each roll will make. With a plain-paper machine, you could face that problem with each sheet of paper. Therefore, because you will have less jamming and less machine downtime, less of your staff time will be wasted. How do you view this antijam aspect as relevant to your business?

CUSTOMER: Well, it certainly makes sense to me. We don't have enough people to spare someone for servicing the fax machine.

YOU: A lot of customers say that. Also, one point you mentioned was your concern about your organization's image as represented by copies on plain paper. That certainly is an important concern with a copy machine, but there is a significant difference between a copier and a fax machine. The fax machine only copies messages you receive, not ones you send out. Since these copies are for your own use and the customers rarely, if ever, see them, you will not have a problem of image.

Step 5. Ask if concern is answered.

YOU: Does that answer your concern about coated-paper copies?

CUSTOMER: Yes.

Step 6. Ask for customer action.

YOU: Would you like the machine delivered tomorrow morning or tomorrow afternoon?

CUSTOMER: Any time after 9:30 will be okay.

Situation Example

You work for a local business machine dealer selling a generic desktop computer system to a small public accounting firm. You have just finished your presentation.

CUSTOMER: Thank you for your time. You have a good piece of equipment, but we're going to buy from [name of big company].

Step 1. Find out the customer's specific concern.

YOU: I wonder why.

CUSTOMER: Well, we feel more confident going with a larger firm that has a national reputation for providing good product and service.

(Since the customer just told you he is not going to buy your product because you are a small company, you don't need step 2.)

Step 3. Is this the only reason?

YOU: Is that the only reason why you will not buy our product?

CUSTOMER: Yes.

YOU: You mean if my product was sold by the big company and the big company's product was sold by me, you'd still buy the product sold by the big company?

CUSTOMER: Well, that is hypothetical, but the answer is yes.

YOU: I'm glad you said that; it means that you have a lot of respect for my product and your concern is primarily about service, is that so?

CUSTOMER: Yes.

YOU: You mean if I can guarantee you in some way that our service is as good as if not better than the large company's service, you would use our product?

CUSTOMER: Yes.

Step 4. Answer the concern.

YOU: Well, I can tell you that since we are a small company, your business means a lot more to us than it does to the big company. Gaining or losing a customer to us means a lot more than it does to them. I can also tell you that we know we provide better service because we are local and the same people who install the equipment actually repair it. We know our customers on a first-name basis, which is different from the big company, which has a rotating service staff. But I have one demonstration I'd like to make to you to convince you that you are more important to us than to the big company. Who in your department contacted [name of big company] and us to request the demonstrations?

CUSTOMER: My secretary.

YOU: Would you please ask your secretary to step in here for a moment?

CUSTOMER: Certainly. (Asks secretary to come into the office.)

YOU: We were just discussing a recent demonstration you had with [big company], and I understand you were the one who made the arrangements with them. Can I ask you a question? When you called [big company], did you reach the person you wanted to speak to the first time, and were you able to get the information you wanted each time you called?

SECRETARY: Well, actually I left messages a few times before somebody got back to me, and it took about four calls to arrange the demonstration.

YOU: Could you compare that to your efforts to contact my company for a demonstration?

SECRETARY: Well, you folks responded after the first call, and there was no mix-up in communication.

YOU: Thank you very much. (Turning to the customer) If that is the kind of difficulties you have in getting attention from [big company] even before you buy the product, can you imagine what it is going to be like after you buy the product? As a customer, you can make the choice of being a small and unimportant customer to a very big company or a very important customer to a very small company, which is us.

Step 5. Ask if concern is answered.

YOU: Does that answer your concern about service?

CUSTOMER: Yes.

Step 6. Ask for customer action.

YOU: How many machines can we deliver?

CUSTOMER: One for each of our staff units.

Situation Example

You are selling electrical mechanical devices to distributors that sell directly to maintenance and construction firms. You have just finished your presentation on a new labor-saving device.

CUSTOMER: Your product is very interesting, but the economy is slowing us down. Come back and show it to me again in 6 months.

Step 1. Find out the customer's specific concern.

YOU: Why do you say that?

CUSTOMER: Well, I don't have to tell you that the construction industry is in a slump, and we're trying to keep our inventories as low as possible.

Step 2. Find out if it is an obstacle to the sale.

YOU: How does that affect this product?

CUSTOMER: We are not going to stock new items that may not move.

Step 3. Is this the only reason?

YOU: Is your concern that this new item may not sell the only reason why you would not stock our product now?

CUSTOMER: It certainly is a good product, but everybody coming in here has good products; now is not the time to add to our inventory.

Step 4. Answer the concern.

YOU: I certainly agree with your concern about inventories in these hard times, but I see you continue to buy some items. I wonder why.

Note: This sounds as though you are still learning about the customer's problem, but you have been in this situation before and you are asking these questions to isolate the problem in the customer's mind.

CUSTOMER: We still buy those items that are in demand and that move off the shelf quickly.

YOU: So it appears that your concern is not about inventory in general but about inventory that is not going to move. Is that right?

CUSTOMER: Yes.

YOU: I'm glad to hear you say that, because the item we're talking about has really been designed to be a fast mover, even in bad times. As I mentioned to you before, the special feature of this item is that it actually eliminates four steps in installation which reduces installation time by 50 percent (benefit). From a contractor's point of view, it actually saves them money (benefit) because they get more work done with fewer people. Another point I was just about to explain is that we have a special counter-top display that highlights the features and benefits of this item which adds to impulse sales at the counter. Our experience with these counter displays with other dealers is that installers have been selecting our item two out of three times versus the items from company A, company B, and company C. So the important question here is not whether you're going to add to inventory but whether you're going to replace current inventory of slow-moving items with these items that will actually move faster.

Let me ask you a hypothetical question—if, for example, you had this item in stock a month ago and you found that your customers were selecting this item two out of three times over similar items in your inventory, would you stop carrying this item or the items from companies A, B, and C?

CUSTOMER: Probably the A, B, and C items.

Step 5. Ask if concern is answered.

YOU: That was exactly the philosophy behind our company's engineering efforts to design this item—to replace less efficient devices. So, in line with your efforts to decrease inventory, if you stock our item, which will give you an increased volume of business, you can also decrease your inventory of those slower-moving items. Does that help with your concern about inventory?

CUSTOMER: Yes.

Step 6. Ask for customer action.

YOU: Do you want to start with the two-pack display or the four-pack display?

CUSTOMER: Let's start with the two-pack display.

10. As mentioned earlier, you will not be faced with an unlimited number of customer concerns in this category blocking the sale. If your manager has not already done so, ask him or her to collect from all the other sales reps a list of concerns customers express as negative aspects for buying your product. Also request that all the best (most effective) answers for those concerns be collected.

    Write out exactly how you will phrase your answers for each concern, and use a tape recorder to practice, practice, practice. Of all the critical "moments of truth" in the selling process when you can win or lose the sale, this is the most frequent point when sales are lost. Most salespeople are unable to satisfactorily answer the customer's concerns about negative aspects of buying your product.

11. In spite of how well you know your product and how good a job you do in presenting it, you will lose some sales because you are unable to satisfy the customer's concern for things beyond your control. For example, if there is no differentiation between your product or service, including terms of sales, delivery, reliability, product image, etc., and the competitive product costs less, you will lose the sale unless you lie or beg. (It's okay to beg, but it's not okay to lie.) But don't lose the sale because you didn't know what the answer was or you delivered a wrong or incomplete answer in a confusing manner that did not satisfy the customer's concern.

12. Sometimes the customer will indicate that other people are also involved in the decision to reject your product, as follows:

    - We have decided...
    - We feel...
    - The committee thinks...
    - We have reviewed your proposal and...

When you hear this, do not proceed with the above process because you will be wasting your time. The customer has just told you that you are not talking to the decision maker. If you had collected the right information from your customer initially, you would have discovered this problem sooner and you would have done your selling to the committee. Your only chance of salvaging this sale is to initiate your selling process to the committee.

PART 6

How to Avoid Losing Sales by Helping Customers to Buy

19

They Think
Something Else
Is More Important

Frequently salespeople tell me that they can't get appointments because customers say they are too busy. Salespeople also complain that when they sell a product which requires the customers to take specific action to advance the sale or to prepare for the receipt or use of the product, the customers do not do their job. They don't get necessary approvals, or send out notices, or schedule support services, or initiate required legal documents, or notify other people affected by the purchase, or get a purchase order number, etc. They know they are supposed to do it because it was discussed, but they do it late or not at all. The customer comments you hear are:

I forgot.

We don't have time to get into that now.

We're going through too many changes now to be involved in this.

I'm sorry I can't see you. I'm spending all my time in meetings because of this reorganization.

This is budget planning time. I'll be lucky if I see my family in the next 2 weeks.

I am sorry. I have been too busy this week to update the credit report I promised.

Listen, this week I'm getting ready to go on vacation, so you will have to wait for your specifications until I get back in three weeks.

I'm sorry. I will definitely mail the signed authorization to you on Monday.

From the salesperson's point of view, the customer's priorities are mixed up. But sometimes the things the customer thinks are more important would not be in question. Such as:

We had a fire in our refinery, and all our capital expenditures are going into that this year, and so we won't be buying any new office equipment from you.

OR

I am trying to hire a new secretary, and so I will not have any time available to see any salespeople for at least 2 weeks.

OR

I'm calling you to cancel tomorrow's appointment to go over specifications because our vice president will be visiting our regional office.

When customers tell you they don't have time to see you or don't have time to listen to your product presentations or to do what they promised to do, they are telling you that *they think something else is more important* than what is on your mind. These can be problems and emergencies that disrupt the daily routine; surprise visits by inspectors, auditors, or bosses; unscheduled meetings; personal problems; severe weather conditions; strikes; breakdowns; resignations; firings; month-end or year-end panics; political infighting; etc. Depending upon your product, you may encounter the customer who thinks the under-the-table pay he is getting for buying your competitor's product is more important than buying your product. Several salespeople who sell pacemakers to doctors once told me that the only way they could get a doctor to use their pacemakers was to equal the competition's under-the-table pay to the doctor. From the customer's point of view, he or she has placed what you do or sell in a relatively lower priority than the other things demanding attention in the same time period.

There is an unwritten law in business, and perhaps in life as well, which is "If something is visible, you can be held accountable for it; if something is invisible, you can't be held accountable for it." Most car owners will spend more time washing and polishing their car than they will in checking their tires or battery. In business, people tend to devote more attention to getting reports to the boss on time than dealing with things that will make the business more profitable, more effective, or even safer. After all, if they don't get that report in, somebody will be on the phone screaming about a late report; but no one will know about a lot of the other things that didn't get done today. The difficulty you have is that the product or service you're trying to sell may not have as visible an effect on the world as other things your customer has to pay attention to.

A few years ago when I was trying to sell a performance appraisal design program to one large company, the customer (a vice president) said, "I like what you have to offer, but we don't want to rock the boat right now." When I asked him what he meant by that, he explained that they had recently spent a year and $100,000 working with another consultant who redesigned their current corporatewide management performance appraisal program. But after the first 6 months of its use, his staff concluded that it was ineffective. He agreed that my design was what they needed, but since they had gone through so much effort introducing the new program, they would have to wait for another 2 years before they tried to introduce a change. In this situation, harmony was more important to the customer than improving quality. I also suspect his personal reputation would be at stake if he had to admit to a $100,000 fiasco.

A salesperson working for an employment agency once told me that he could not understand why one of his customers, a regional manager from a worldwide business machine company, refused for four months to hire salespeople although there were four vacant territories in his region. Eventually the salesperson discovered the reason: The regional manager did not try to fill the sales vacancies because he was trying to reduce expenses so he would get the largest possible bonus based on his year's financial performance. Because of the way his company calculated bonuses, the regional manager discovered that the cost savings from not having four salespeople on the payroll would produce more bonus than any sales gain that could have been achieved by adding four new salespeople in the last four months of his fiscal year. You may think that this manager's action was dishonest, selfish, misguided, or downright stupid, but nevertheless we are talking about the real world and it must have seemed like a good idea to this customer.

People in life in general always have to make decisions in their allocation of the resources they control, whatever those resources are—time, money, or even emotional concern. In the pharmaceutical industry it is quite common for the sales representatives to leave samples for the doctor to use on patients. On follow-up sales calls when the sales representative asks the doctor if he or she used the samples, a common response from the doctor is, "I forgot."

Salespeople don't realize that although today's sale is a big part of their life, it is only one small part among many in the customer's daily life. Our customers are busy people with more things to be done in a day than can be done in a day. They have their own daily goals and plans which get displaced by daily work pressures, phone calls, and panics which must be handled. The promise they make to you to do something drops in priority or is totally forgotten soon after you leave their office. We are all faced with this waterfall of things we plan to do each day along with meeting the requests and demands of our bosses, friends, and loved ones. Some things go undone because a person cannot do everything within the time constraints. Your problem as a salesperson is that customers frequently choose to do what they think is important in contrast to what you think is important.

Solution

1. *Managing the sale* in this situation is a big challenge because of the minimal control you have over the customer when you

are not present. If you can do the things you need the customer to do, such as filling out forms, bring the forms with you and fill them out yourself. Ask your customer if you can have her secretary type something you need. If you can do some things that need to be done by working with someone else in the organization, do it. If you can get the customer to do the needed things while you are there, do it. If other people are needed to decide something, have them present in the meeting.

2. When customers promise to do things, ask, "Is there anything you can think of which might occur which could prevent you from doing that?" If they mention some things, discuss how you (both) will work around those problems.

3. Don't assume customers will do what they promised to do or you will always discover too late that they have not done so. You must follow up on the specific things customers promise to do when they promised to do them. But don't make it an interrogation; i.e., "I called to find out if you did _____." Make it a friendly conversation that ends with "By the way, John, you were planning to send your lease agreement to me yesterday. I was wondering if you did that."

4. If it is customary for customers to tell you they didn't do things because they forgot, you have to do something to help them remember. If a customer promises to use samples in your absence, get him to tell you when he plans to use them—on which day of which week or for what particular situation. If you are selling to a doctor and she promises to use your sample on a patient, get her to write the name of the patient right on the box of your sample or ask her permission to get the nurse to put a note in that patient's folder so that when the doctor opens it, she will see the reminder that she planned to use your sample.

It is okay to call customers at the time they said they were going to use your samples or perform a specific task and remind them that they had said they were going do that. Some salespeople find it effective to send greeting cards to their customers as reminders of what they had promised to do.

5. When a customer has not done something because of changed priorities (he thinks something else is more important), his choices are out of balance. Do one of the following:

   a. Try to change the priorities.

   OR

   b. Find a solution around the priorities problem.

   - If you choose *a* as your action, you have to help the customer understand the value (cost-benefit) of his choices.

Situation Example

CUSTOMER: I'm going on vacation, and so I cannot give you the specifications you want until I return in 3 weeks.

YOU: (After discussing the intended vacation) You know, if I could get those specifications before you leave, we could have the new system up and running 3 weeks sooner, which would mean a saving to your company of $300 per week, or almost a total of $1000. Is there any way to get those specs to me before you leave?

Situation Example

CUSTOMER: We are on a tight budget with limits on what we buy, so I don't want to waste your time or mine on a sales call.

YOU: It sounds as though you folks are trying to be more efficient in how you spend your time.

CUSTOMER: You're right on target.

YOU: That's music to my ears, because most of our customers are interested in our system as an economical move—it saves them money. I'm going to be in the area anyhow. What is a good time for you on Wednesday to show you some of our money-saving ideas?

In this approach, the thing that you're selling is not your product, but the idea that the priorities should change. The chance to save $300 per week and the idea that money-saving services or products are more critical during hard times than during good times should be seen as value when choosing between priorities.

   - If you choose *b* as your action, you have to help the customer find ways around these unbalanced priorities. Since you can't change the priorities, work around them or get someone else in the customer's organization to do what the customer is not doing.

Situation Example

CUSTOMER: I'm calling to cancel our appointment tomorrow to go over specifications because our vice president will be visiting our regional office.

YOU: I'm sorry you have to cancel. If I don't have the specs, I can't submit your order. That could mean your delivery date will not be met.

CUSTOMER: It can't be helped.

YOU: What time will the VP arrive?

CUSTOMER: We don't know exactly, but it will be in the afternoon sometime. But it is a madhouse around here trying to get things in shape.

YOU: I can understand the hassle you're in, and I think I can help. You have to eat lunch anyhow, and since I am going to be in the area, I will bring over some sandwiches and we can eat in your office and clear up the specs at the same time. Do you like roast beef or ham and cheese, and what do you want to drink?

Situation Example

CUSTOMER: I know I promised you an updated credit report this week, but I am going to be locked into meetings all week. You are going to have to wait until next week.

YOU: I am sorry to hear that things are so hectic for you. I know you make up that report, but do you have the data or do they come from accounting?

CUSTOMER: They come from accounting, but I have to update the report and sign it.

YOU: I have an idea that will save you time and still help us get your order to you on time. Give me the name of someone in accounting who has all the numbers, and I will see him tomorrow and together we will update the report. All you will have to do is sign it. Whom should I contact in accounting?

20

They Don't Know How to Make the Buying Decision

This probably sounds strange to you as a reason why you wouldn't get a sale. After all, what's for them to know? They give you their money, you give them your product, and the deal is done. Nothing could be simpler for the customer than to say, "I'll take it." If you're selling shoes, it seems logical enough for the customer to know what he or she has to do to be able to walk out of the store with new shoes. But have you ever been in a restaurant and you wanted to pay your bill after your meal and you had to ask, "Do I pay you, or do I pay the cashier?" This seems like a small problem which doesn't last too long. But let's look at how this situation escalates as reasons for losing sales when the buying process is more convoluted.

In most selling situations buyers are not merely dealing with one source for a product or service. Most business organizations require people making buying decisions to get three or more competitive quotes so that the final buying decision results in getting the best product under the best conditions. One difficulty buyers face is that different companies selling the same product do not describe the product in the same way. For example, a buyer evaluating six proposals for group health insurance, submitted by six different companies, will be unable to make an item-by-item comparison because of the way each insurance company structures its group plan. Not only will companies vary the amount they pay by surgical procedure, but they will also include or exclude certain types of surgery. For example, one may include cosmetic surgery for any reason, and the other will include it only for accidents. All the plans may include dental care, but it is difficult to make a direct comparison between each dental plan because of each company's variation on how it provides the 30 or 40 different aspects of each dental plan. One company's dental plan may include bridgework as a normal procedure, but another may only include bridgework as reconstruction surgery following damage. The same thing applies in buying computers, with variations in the size and color of the screen, convenience of the keyboard, availability of maintenance, amount of training required before an operator becomes proficient, memory capacity, size of the hardware itself, speed, availability of software, and potential of obsolescence. I run into the same confusion when I want to purchase new tires for my car. The salespeople use industry jargon I don't understand and quote studies that may or may not be independent and may or may not be true.

People look at many products when they're trying to make the buying decision, and it is not as simple as comparing apples with apples; the buyer gets confused.

One woman told me that she has delayed her purchase of a microwave oven for 3 years because she has trouble deciding which one to buy. Each manufacturer has its own little features; therefore, no two ovens are the same. A retailer who sells hiking equipment told me that customers buying hiking boots for the first time have difficulty deciding what to buy. He said they don't even know how to decide which one fits better because hiking boots fit differently than do other kinds of shoes. Additionally, it gets more complicated deciding whether they should buy high-tops or medium cuts, leather or nylon, single or double tongue, lightweight not waterproof or heavyweight waterproof. Some of the customers don't even know what kind of socks to wear with hiking boots. He said if you don't take the customers in hand and find out exactly what kind of hiking they plan to do and what kind of socks they plan to wear, they either buy nothing at all or buy the wrong boot and blame you for a bad decision when they return from their trip.

A retailer who sells fishing equipment tells a similar story about inexperienced buyers outfitting themselves for their first fishing trip. Some car buyers have the same difficulty deciding between models—one is larger, but the other one is faster; one is sporty, but the other one is less expensive to operate; one has the right color, but the other one is easier to keep clean; one is less expensive, but the other one has more safety features and a better stereo system.

These are not dumb customers; they are merely customers who don't know how to make the buying decision. If the salesperson on the other end of this customer situation does not *manage the sale*, the result will be "no sale."

Solution

1. When customers are confused about making the buying decision, you can *manage the sale* by helping them make product comparisons to eliminate that confusion. To be able to do that you must educate yourself about your competitors' products. You must be able to explain the differences in features and benefits and the differences in conditions of purchase, such as pricing structure, method of paying, packaging, method of delivery, service support, etc.

2. Customers are better able to make buying decisions when they clearly understand their needs. With new products you have to help them do that. So use your questioning techniques to identify what the customer needs before making product comparisons.

3. With each customer find out what products he or she is considering along with yours so that you know whether you are in a strong or weak competitive position. When you know what you have to sell against, plan your presentation around product comparisons.

4. When summarizing your product at the end of your presentation, always refer to the needs list: "You said you were

looking to solve _____ , and as I pointed out, our product supplies _____ (benefit). You also said you're very interested in having _____ occur, and in the study I showed you we are very strong in producing _____ effect."

5. When the customer says, "I'm not sure what I should do," your response should be, "Let me help you in your analysis." Proceed by listing the needs you previously identified and explaining at each point how your product satisfies those needs. After presenting each point, ask, "Does the other product you've seen do this for you?"

6. Forecast the questions customers will ask you in comparing your product with competitive products. For example, if a customer has seen a competitive product that in fact is made better than your product, what is your answer when she says, "Yesterday I saw your competitor's product which is better constructed than yours; they use cast iron where you use cast aluminum"? (See Chapter 14, "They Are Afraid to Buy.")

7. If a competitive product the customer is considering is stronger than your product in only a few points—but not in the majority—point that out to the customer.

8. If the competitive product is stronger in more ways than yours, do not make a feature-by-feature comparison. Say, "There are products on the market which are equally as good and it is difficult to make a choice, but the reason why you should buy my product is _____ ," and point out the few strong points of your product. When you are finished, ask the customer to take action.

9. If you can't get the sale today because the customer plans to look at other competitive products, the only thing you can do is to set the standard of comparison for the customer. You can say, "To help you make a fair comparison, let's make up a list of the points you think are important." You will actually be setting the specifications that your product can successfully meet but that other products may not meet.

Some salespeople who have difficulty selling their products to builders and contractors because of the confusion in comparing products change their selling strategy. They call on architects to establish product specifications that mirror the features and benefits of their products. For example, one floor-covering manufacturer has a "no-stain" feature exclusive to its product. The manufacturer salesperson is assured of getting the business when the architect includes the "no-stain" feature in specifications because no other company can meet this specification.

10. Stay in contact with the customer while competitive products are being reviewed to make sure you don't lose the sale. You can even ask the customer, "Will you please do me a favor? I know you're looking at a lot of other products, but please let me meet with you before you make your final decision."

21

They Don't Know How to Sell

Picture this situation. On your last sales call after you complete your presentation, the customer tells you that he likes your product and wants to buy it, but he has to get approval from upper management. You walk out of the customer's office with a smile on your face because the sale looks like a sure thing. But when you meet with him a week later, he gives you the sad news, "I couldn't get upper management to go along." Another lost sale, and it doesn't seem fair. After all, you did your job right, but some upper-level management bozo sticks his nose in it and fouls up the sale. How much is a poor hard-working salesperson expected to do; a person can't do everything.

Well, you are right—a person can't be expected to do everything. But if you want to be successful in selling, you must do everything that is needed to be done to get the sale. This sale was not lost because you didn't do something right. It was lost because you didn't do enough of the right things. You did not deal with the obstacle staring you in the face. You lost this sale because your customer could not sell (convince) upper management the same way you sold your customer. In all situations, when you are unable to face the final decision maker, you will lose some sales because the person talking to the final decision maker cannot do what you do; he does not know how to sell. This person is failing to sell to the decision maker for the same reasons you could fail in your selling job; he doesn't know how

to do it. When the customer says he will have to send your proposal to someone else or must present your proposal to a committee, the selling process is shifting from you to someone else.
You should be as concerned about that as you would be in
lending your brand-new Porsche to someone who does not yet
know how to drive. In both situations you will probably lose
money.

Solution

1. One of the top-10 reasons why salespeople lose sales is
   because they do not talk to the decision maker. One early
   step in *managing the sale* is finding out who actually makes
   the buying decision and deal with that person.

2. When it seems impossible for you to talk to the decision
   makers, ask your manager for assistance. Frequently decision makers who will not talk to a salesperson will talk to a
   sales manager. Your manager can open the door for you, but
   you will do the follow-up selling.

3. Sometimes the only way to meet decision makers is to get
   them out of their shells by inviting them to what appears to
   be a meeting of other important people. This could be a
   meeting or cocktail party for a special showing of your product. If you use a formal invitation, the impression of exclu-
   sivity gets their attention.

4. If you can't talk to committees, talk to committee members
   individually.

5. If you normally present your product to individuals but now
   you are going to present it to a group or committee, you
   must change your presentation. Speaking to groups requires
   different speech techniques and visual aids than speaking to
   individuals. For example, you can hold up a typewritten
   sheet of information for a single customer to see, but it
   would not work in a room with 10 people.

6. If it is impossible to deal directly with the decision maker,
   you must train your messenger. Do not attempt to make this

person into a salesperson, because you will not have time to do that. But help this person organize the material in sequence and format, with emphasis on benefits, so that it will deal with the known customer concerns in an understandable and convincing way. You and your direct contact must forecast the decision maker's questions or concerns and formulate the most effective answers.

To be certain that the sale doesn't rely on the speech-making skills of your contact, who is probably not a trained speech maker, give him a fail-safe approach using graphics (slides, posters, charts) and handouts that are self-explanatory and that will support the presentation.

If your proposal is being forwarded in writing instead of being presented orally, work with your contact to make sure the written proposal does everything you want it to do as a selling message.

Make sure that the "deal" your messenger is delivering to the decision maker is complete, with all terms and conditions of sale spelled out so a decision can be made. As always, your deal should not present the decision maker with a choice to buy or not buy your product, but with the choice of how to buy it, i.e., cash or credit, monthly or annual billing, 100 cases or a carload, with or without service contracts, etc.

7. Whether or not you did the right things above, when the customer says, "I couldn't get upper management to go along," use questioning techniques to find out why—a good first question is, "I wonder why?"

22

They Don't Know How to Order

It would be very unusual for a customer to tell you, "I never did this before, and so I don't know exactly what to buy." In fact, as we get older in life, we soon discover that when you announce to the world that you don't know what you are doing, it is the signal for someone to take advantage of you. You become what Barnum said was born every minute, a sucker. However, in any situation you can be a sucker only once, because being taken advantage of teaches you what not to do the next time.

If the customer has never ordered your product before, he may not know:

- The assorted sizes to order
- The right packaging among choices available
- The correct quantities because the product turns bad sitting on the shelf
- The most economical method of shipping
- The proper sequence of getting delivery of materials
- The most economical terms for buying
- The appropriate contract arrangements (1 month or 1 year)
- Whether to pay for it all in advance, to pay only upon delivery, or to make partial payments as the shipments arrive

- How much extra to buy because of a percentage loss due to the (production, shipping, aging) process

Last year the owner of a small manufacturing company told me about his unpleasant buying experience when he first started in business, manufacturing ground-level trampolines for outdoor use. Because he didn't have much money, he designed his own trampolines and bought the steel, canvas, and nylon webbing to build them himself. He said he knew nothing about buying nylon webbing or canvas and had explained that to the salesman selling the canvas. After agreeing to buying 60 feet of canvas, which was exactly what he needed for his first six experimental models, he was surprised that the salesman accompanied him to the warehouse where his order was measured very precisely to the inch. He assumed that the salesman was taking a special interest in what might become a future valued customer. To make a long story short, when the entrepreneur finished making his fifth trampoline, he discovered that there was not enough canvas left to finish the sixth trampoline. He knew he had bought enough canvas because he saw it measured to the inch and he hadn't wasted any in manufacturing. He called the salesman to ask if the salesman had any ideas about what had happened. The salesman informed him that canvas always shrinks when it's removed from its original roll. When the entrepreneur asked the salesman why he had not mentioned that, the salesman said, "You didn't ask." The entrepreneur went on to explain that his business has gotten much bigger since then and he no longer makes trampolines, but he has never purchased any more supplies from the company that sold the canvas.

Many customers lured by big discounts on volume purchases buy more product than they actually need. The result is cash is tied up unnecessarily and occasionally the product deteriorates on the shelf. The salesperson may have gotten a large commission for a large sale, but it will be the last sale she will get out of that customer.

You will not usually lose a sale the first time because a customer did not know how to order, but you will most likely lose the second sale to that customer because you didn't deal appropriately with this problem the first time around.

Solution

1. Understand that part of *managing the sale* is protecting customers from doing dumb things. It is your job to educate them about the vagaries, advantages, and disadvantages of the quantity, form, and format of your product and the conditions under which they purchase your product. It is not enough to honestly answer their questions; you must give them information they need but may not ask for to make a good buying decision.

2. Do a *complete* customer analysis so that you will not make the mistake of letting the customer do the wrong thing.

3. If the customer will not follow your advice when purchasing your product and you know it is self-destructive behavior, notify the customer in writing to get it on record that you tried to do the right thing. This will prevent him from blaming you when he later discovers his foolish action.

23

They Don't Know How to Use Your Product

From a salesperson's point of view, it might seem logical that if you sell a good product and you don't abuse the customer on price or quantity or other terms, your job is done; from then on, if things don't go well, it's the customer's problem. It may also seem reasonable that if your product requires technical installation or support that is provided by other people in your organization, once the product is sold, it's no longer your problem. But this would be a reasonable point of view only if you never wanted to sell to the same customer again and you don't mind if your marketplace shrinks because of what unhappy customers tell their friends. Unhappy customers are very bad for business. I've heard the following comments from unhappy customers:

It never seemed to work right from the day we got it, so we just gave up on it.

Yes, it's supposed to do a good job, but most of the people are afraid to use it.

Yes, we've had it for a year now, but we're still struggling to make it work for us.

No, we are not using it. When we bought it, we didn't realize all the other changes we'd have to make to be able to use it; and we can't afford to make all those other changes right now.

From their point of view, these customers did not get what they paid for. And this problem can be caused by questions the customer can't answer:

How do we dispose of the old equipment?

How do we cancel the old contract?

How do we prepare the work area for the new equipment?

I know you will train our current employees, but who will train our future new hires?

Must we hire new people who know how to operate your system?

How long does it take to set up the equipment after we receive it?

What changes do we have to make to our system to be able to use your equipment?

How do I apply for a government permit to operate your product?

Sometimes customers face delays in utilizing your equipment because they do not properly prepare for its delivery. Required preparation can include everything from operator training to changes in the work environment, such as floating floors, controlled temperatures, dust-free clean rooms, special heavy-duty concrete foundations, special soundproofing, or fire-protection facilities. Sometimes it may be necessary to hire new employees to use new equipment because no one on staff has the necessary experience. The buyer may have to set up special waste disposal facilities not previously needed.

In some situations, the amount of preparation required to be able to use the new product increases costs beyond the initial purchase price. When customers don't correctly understand this in advance, they feel they have been burned by you. You will lose repeat business with customers in this situation and new sales with other customers who know how badly this customer was treated.

Solution

1. Include as part of your needs analysis with each customer the amount of preparation that will be needed to use your product. This is crucial when your type of product has never been used by this customer.

2. Make sure the customer is aware of all changes, preparation, and costs involved in the purchasing decision. Include not only the initial purchase price, but capital expenditure for preparation as well as service requirements to use what you are selling.

3. After the purchase has been made, help your customer create a step-by-step plan of things that must be done in preparation to use your product or service. If there are service people in your organization who normally work with customers in preparation for delivery, you will have to spend less time on the details, but make sure there is a plan.

4. Follow up with the customer to be sure the preparation plan is being followed by the customer's people, as well as your service people. When things are not happening, get involved and look for ways around the stoppage. You have to *manage the sale* so you don't get burned.

24

They Don't Know How to Negotiate

This only happens with customers who are unfamiliar with buying what you are selling. It could be their first experience in making any purchase. You know you face this problem when the sales call ends immediately after you announce the price of your product. The customer asked you how much, you told her the price, and she said, "It's too much," and ended the meeting. In the next instant you're out on the sidewalk talking to yourself:

Doesn't she know she can make an offer?

Doesn't she know she can ask me if there's a discount for quantity?

Doesn't she know she can ask me, "Is that your best price?"

Doesn't she know she can ask me, "Is there any way we can get the price down?"

The answer is that the customer doesn't know she can ask those questions. This naive buyer believes that when she asked you the price, you told her the one and only price. She doesn't know that there is the list price, the asking price, and a final price. She doesn't know the rule of life, "Everyone negotiates price." In fact, if you're selling products to people who usually negotiate, you will have a problem if you quote your best price first. That price becomes your beginning point for negotiation, and you will end up selling the product for less than what you intended or lose the sale.

Solution

1. If you've never met this customer before, do not assume that she knows how to negotiate. Find out something about her background and her buying experience, and listen to how she asks questions. If she says, "What is your asking price?" or "What is your list price?" you can assume she knows there is a difference between these and the selling price. Give the answer she asks for.

2. When the customer asks the price of your product, you have just moved into the closing mode of your selling process. The customer is telling you he wants to own your product and is trying to find out how much it will cost to achieve that goal. Ask those questions that will move the sale forward. Start by saying, "Since the price depends on a lot of variables, could I ask you a few more questions that will help you get the best price?" These questions will lead the customer through the buying decision and will help you get to the right answer concerning price.

   - How many do you want?
   - What are the specifications?
   - How do you want them delivered?
   - How will you pay? (The difference between cash or credit sometimes determines the price.)
   - How long do you want the buying agreement to be in effect?

   You can also help the customer negotiate by explaining how price may vary with changes in the specifications and order quantities.

3. Before the customer asks you your price, you should have learned what competitor products she has previously seen. If you know your competitive information, you will know what price you are competing against so your price will be competitive.

4. There are customers who don't know when to stop negotiating. You can give them your best terms, but they will ask for more. It is understandable that you will lose sales occasionally because customers cannot afford to pay even your lowest price. Since the goal in selling is profitable sales versus sales at any cost, learn to walk away from unprofitable sales. But you don't want to lose any sales when the customer can afford to buy your product but thinks that he cannot. This is not a common problem, but knowing how to *manage the sale* in this situation will prevent an unnecessary lost sale.

PART 7
Conclusion

25

How to Get Your Act Together

Recently during the U.S. Open Tennis Championship a commentator describing a player said, "He has a lot of talent, but he doesn't have it together." And it struck me that a lot of salespeople suffer from the same problem: They have a lot of talent and are working hard but are not making progress. It's obvious that the reason why customers don't do what you want them to do is because salespeople either fail to do the right thing or actually do the wrong thing to customers. To be successful in selling, not only do you have to do the right things, but you have to do them at the right time; you have to "get it together."

When training sales managers, one of the questions I ask each group is, "Why are salespeople in your business not as successful as they could be?" Over the last 20 years I've collected answers from several thousand managers across all product lines, including pharmaceuticals, financial products, specialty foods, cosmetics, insurance, business machines, home decorations, alcoholic beverages, clothing, packaging materials, insecticides, and chemicals. Although there was slight variation in emphasis by industry, all the reasons given were quite similar. Below is a list of these reasons categorized according to when they occur in the selling process—as pre-sales call, during the sales call, and post-sales call.

21 Reasons Why Salespeople Fail

Pre-Sales Call

1. *Has no sales call objective.* The salesperson has no clear understanding of what he wants to accomplish on the sales call. There is no customer action objective (CAO) for each and every sales call.

2. *Calls on the wrong customers.* The salesperson wastes time calling on customers who don't need the product; or who would buy in such small quantities that the sale would have little impact on total sales result; or for whom the product either is inadequate to meet the customer's needs or provides grossly more benefits than the customer needs or can afford to buy.

3. *Does not plan each sales presentation.* The salesperson enters the world of the customer willing to do anything but prepared to do nothing specific. Either the salesperson gives the same presentation like a parrot to all customers, or else gives no presentation but instead carries on a pointless, rambling discussion that only wastes time and leads nowhere. This usually occurs because the salesperson didn't have a call objective.

4. *Avoids customers who are difficult.* The salesperson calls on customers who are pleasant to call on rather than go where there is sales potential. Customers who are difficult to see or who ask too many questions or who argue are avoided regardless of the potential sale that could be derived from that customer.

5. *Does not know competitive information.* The salesperson doesn't have sufficient and accurate information about the competitor's product and pricing, therefore, believable comparisons between products cannot be made.

6. *Has no call frequency.* With most products, multiple sales calls are required both to get a first sale and to maintain continuing sales from an existing customer. The salesperson

who doesn't plan a call frequency has no plan of selling activities. He sees some customers too frequently and other customers not frequently enough.

7. *Does not work a full day.* This salesperson arrives in her territory late, takes long lunches, and leaves early. Effective use of time is one of the biggest separators between highly successful and unsuccessful salespeople. If you are the best salesperson in the world but your poor use of time prevents you from seeing as many customers as you could, the result will be lower sales for you and your organization by week, by month, by year.

During the Sales Call

8. *Does not talk to the decision maker.* This salesperson does not verify whether or not the person he is talking to can make the buying decision, and so he wastes time making sales presentations to people who cannot buy.

9. *Does not establish customer needs.* This salesperson does not know how to use questioning techniques to uncover the customer's needs—or does not try because her sales presentation concentrates on "selling" as opposed to helping the customer to buy.

10. *Presents the wrong products.* The salesperson presents products that may have wonderful benefits, but none of them relate to this particular customer. Oddly enough, he may have products that actually fit this customer's needs, but they are not presented. This reason is usually related to reason 9.

11. *Does not use sales aids effectively.* This salesperson varies from using no sales aids, to using the wrong sales aids, to using sales aids ineffectively. For example, information from printed materials has not been memorized, therefore, she must read the information losing eye contact. She uses sales aids as proof when proof isn't needed, or does not use any proof when it is needed, or uses the wrong sales aid that is not related to the customer's question or point of concern.

Frequently she flubs product demonstrations by making errors or misspeaking and may give samples to the customer without getting any promises from the customer to use them.

12. *Does not talk about benefits.* The salesperson invariably does not know the difference between a product feature and a customer benefit. He spends time talking about the wonderful features of the product but does not translate how the customer will benefit from these features.

13. *Does not permit the customer to respond.* The salesperson gives speeches rather than holding conversations with customers, and her objective is to finish the presentation as soon as possible. It seems as though this salesperson would like to say to the customer, "Please stop interrupting me with your questions. I'm trying to get finished with my sales presentation, so I can get out of here."

14. *Can't answer questions about the product.* The salesperson either gives misinformation or frequently says, "I don't know," "I'm not sure," "I'll check on that," "Possibly," or "I think." He cannot answer the customer's questions because he is unfamiliar with the product and its application.

15. *Can't handle objections.* The salesperson is unable to deal with the customer's doubts and concerns so that they no longer exist as an obstacle to getting the sale. She either does not try or more commonly uses the wrong process and fails.

16. *Does not do things that generate sales for the customer.* This arises as a reason for sales failure only in situations where the salesperson's customer is in a resale situation, such as a retailer or distributor. The product being sold is supposed to help this customer generate more sales to his customers. But the salesperson does not do that. He loads up the customer with inventory or does not give assistance to the customer's sales staff. (This does not relate to the problem of your customer being unable to sell his boss.)

17. *Does not ask for the order.* The salesperson usually works hard, makes good sales presentations, romanticizes the

product, but ends the sales call without asking the customer to take any buying action. She does not ask for the cash or the purchase order, does not ask the customer to choose a color or size, does not ask to make appointments, does not ask for introductions, etc. She does not commonly ask the closing question. If the salesperson does not have a CAO for the call, she will probably not ask the customer to take action.

18. *Does not respond to buying signals.* Buying signals are actions by the customers which indicate that he or she is interested in purchasing the product. Some of these buying signals can be questions, such as "How much does this cost?" or "Is it very expensive?" or "Can I get it in blue?" or "Can you package these 2-up instead of 4-up?" or "Will I be able to finance this purchase?" or "How long does it take to learn how to use it?" These questions clearly indicate that the customer is thinking about owning the product. The customer can also give buying signals that are nonverbal, such as holding the product in ways that it would be used, or examining the product more intensely, or smiling and nodding while looking at the product, or handling the product in a way that indicates approval of its quality or workmanship, etc.

It is generally agreed that when a customer emits a buying signal, the salesperson should begin closing the sale by asking the customer to take a buying action. This salesperson misses the buying signals.

Post-Sales Call

19. *Has poor or no records of what happened on a call.* The salesperson keeps no records of selling activities with customers or else has incomplete or useless records. Highly effective salespeople can look at their customer records and recite the history of the selling progress with each customer. Ineffective salespeople are not aware of a selling history with a customer; therefore, his sales calls are not a series of events which cause the sale to progress. His sales calls are individual and unrelated interventions without a progres-

sive sequence and frequently are repetitions of the previous call which bore customers and do not generate sales. When record keeping is mentioned to this salesperson, the frequent response is, "I can keep it all in my head." But he can't.

20. *Does not analyze the sales call.* The salesperson chooses not to or is unable to analyze a sales call and isolate what was done well and what was done badly. Therefore, she is unable to plan to repeat the good things or avoid repeating the bad things. As mentioned earlier, one secret to success is avoiding doing dumb things repeatedly. This salesperson rarely improves.

21. *Does not follow up.* The salesperson does not respond to requests by the customer or do promised things between sales calls. He may not check on or monitor processes or services performed by other sales support people. He does not check on or monitor the things the customer has promised to do. Some salespeople do not follow up because they assume that things are progressing as they are supposed to progress. But frequently follow-up does not occur because the salesperson cannot control his own activities. Frequent comments by this kind of salesperson include "I forgot," "I was just getting around to that," "Something came up," "Yes, I know I'm late, but I've been busy," and "I assumed things were going according to plan."

These 21 reasons are not the only reasons for lack of sales success, and they don't describe the worst salesperson in the world. Furthermore, I have never known a salesperson who did all these things wrong. It is more common for a salesperson to fail for two or possibly three of the above reasons. Interestingly, the salesperson failing for one or more of the above reasons actually gets sales; he just doesn't get as many sales as he could have gotten. But it only takes one reason to have a dramatic negative effect on your sales performance. Even if you avoid all the above reasons, it doesn't mean that you will get every sale because there are other reasons for failure.

There are situations when you don't make the sale because the customer went out of business, or is buying the product from one of his relatives, or is actually getting an under-the-table payoff from your competition. There are situations when you must give up on a customer because he requires an inordinate amount of your time to be sold. And, of course, there are those occasional selling situations when nothing you do will work. The selling profession is somewhat like life in general—not every day is perfect, and not everything you do, no matter how perfect, will result in a sale. But the secret to success is to avoid losing sales unnecessarily. And you can do that if you approach your job as "selling is the management of buying." You will lose fewer sales than everybody else.

Since you need the customer's cooperation to be successful in selling, your success will be directly related to how much of that customer's cooperation you gain. The exciting part of selling, as well as the confounding part, is that you don't have total control over the customer. Obviously, you can't stick a gun in the customer's ear and say, "Buy my product or else." The other extreme would be merely hoping for success; i.e., "I'll do a lot of things and hope that something might work." The best approach is to maximize the effectiveness of any influence you have over customers. The secret to maximizing your influence is to avoid the conflict posture of "them versus me" and recognize that you and your customers are on the same side; you are helping them to buy. Through the use of situation analysis in this book, you have learned that from the customers' point of view there are logical reasons why they do or do not do what it is you want them to do. If you *manage the sale* by dealing with those reasons successfully, you will have many more customers do what you want them to do.

A Professional Guide to Help You Sell More

By now you should have also concluded that you must become more sensitive to those critical "moments of truth" in selling when your success hinges on your doing the right thing perfectly at that moment in time. You have to stop thinking of your job as calling on three or five or ten customers per day, and start thinking of each sales call as a workday—a separate selling performance. Your aim is to better understand each customer's point of view as unique and avoid saying and doing the same thing in front of every customer without deviation whether or not it's needed and whether or not it works.

As a consultant, I have designed selling guides that have proved highly effective in helping salespeople to pay attention to those critical actions that lead to sales success. To help you, I've created a Professional Selling Guide (included at the end of this chapter) you can use to improve your performance. The guide will prompt you before the sales call to make sure your preparation is correct and complete, and it will guide you in self-analysis after the call, targeting what you did right and what you must improve the next time. And as you now know, preparation and analysis are two key ingredients for professionalism and continuous improvement.

The objective of this self-analysis is for you to achieve your professional goal of continuous improvement. You have my permission to copy the form and make as many copies as you need for your personal use as long as you include the copyright information on your copies. The way to use the Professional Selling Guide is to review the "Pre-call" items before the call to make sure you are prepared for the call. Then review the rest of the items after the call using checkmarks to record your performance. Concentrate on improving those actions you check most frequently in the "Must Improve" column. If you concentrate on your improvement efforts during the day, you should see improvements by the end of each day.

If you begin by using this guide before and after every sales call, you will eventually be able to think of these items without even looking at the guide. As part of your continual improvement, you should keep track of those items that repeatedly fall into the "Must Improve" category. If there's something that you are doing that must improve and that condition doesn't change, it means that you are not progressing.

If there is a certain aspect of your performance you want to improve, ask yourself the question, "What do I have to do differently so that this performance will improve?" Don't be surprised if the repeated answer is, "To study and practice more."

We have come to the end of a detailed analysis of a complicated but important subject. If you have read this book only one
time, you may conclude, "I'll never remember all of this," and
you would be right. The solution is to read it and make notes as
many times as you need to do it. If you have never sold before,
it will be easier for you to learn these techniques of "selling is
the management of buying"—you will not have to break any
bad habits. If you have selling experience, the big difficulty for
you will be to change your point of view of your selling job. If
you asked me to give you one piece of advice to help you each
day, I would say, "Your daily goal should not be to 'sell something today.' It should be to 'help someone buy something
today.'"

I wish you good luck, hard work, and sales success.

Professional Selling Guide

Must
O.K. Improve

Pre-call

Know your product:

- Do you know your product's features?
- Do you know the benefits of each feature by customer situation?
- Do you know all terms of purchase (pricing, delivery schedule, credit terms)?
- Can you demonstrate your product blindfolded?
- Can you recite the information in your sales aids blindfolded?

Know your competitors' products:

- Do you know the features of your competitors' products?
- Do you know the benefits of each competitor's feature?
- Do you know your product's strength over the competitors' features and benefits?
- Do you know competitive pricing and conditions of sale?

Know your customer:

- Do you know about this customer's type of business?
- Do you know this customer's potential for sales?
- Do you know this customer's past history with your company?
- Do you know this customer's past history with you (customer records)?

Be prepared for the call:

- Do you have a customer sales goal for this customer?
- Do you have a CAO for this call?
- Do you have a plan of what *you* will do on this call?
- Do you have all needed sales aids with you?
- Can you pass the blindfold sample case test?
- Have you forecast this customer's concerns?
- Have you practiced how to answer forecast concerns?
- Do you know how you will ask your closing questions?
- Have you checked your equipment today to be sure it works?
- Do you know what you will talk about to establish rapport?
- Do you know what the customer promised to do on the last call?

Check your personal image:

- Hygiene (body, breath, hands, and fingernails)
- Costume—appropriate for the customer's world
- Costume—clean and neat

During the Call

- Did you establish rapport with everyone you met?

	Must
	O.K. Improve

- Did you show interest when the customer spoke? ____ ____
- Did you maintain eye contact? ____ ____
- Did you identify competition, if any? ____ ____
- Did you ask the customer if he or she did what was promised on the last call (use sample, etc.)? ____ ____

Needs:
- Did you uncover customer problems, needs, or desires? ____ ____
- Did you identify the decision maker? ____ ____

Presentation:
- Did you present benefits related to customer needs? ____ ____
- Did you present features to support the benefits? ____ ____
- Did you present proof as needed? ____ ____
- Did you validate the customer's understanding? ____ ____
- Did you ask for the customer's agreement that your benefits will satisfy identified needs? ____ ____
- Did you speak so the customer could understand your words? ____ ____
- Was your presentation organized in logical sequence? ____ ____
- Did you avoid interrupting the customer? ____ ____
- Did you wait for the customer to respond after asking a question? ____ ____
- Did you demonstrate your product without faltering? ____ ____
- Did you use sales aids without losing eye contact? ____ ____
- Did you ask specific questions when the customer's comments were vague? ____ ____

Closing:
- Did you summarize product benefits, if needed? ____ ____
- Did you ask the customer to take action (your CAO)? ____ ____
- Did you follow correct steps when the customer mentioned concerns? ____ ____
- Did you ask for action dates if the customer must do things after you leave? ____ ____

Post-call

- Did your customer take requested action (your CAO)? ____ ____
- Did you analyze the call to know what you did well? ____ ____
- Did you analyze the call to know what you could have done better? ____ ____
- Did you learn anything on this call which will help you in the future? ____ ____
- Should you call on the customer again? ____ ____
- If yes, do you know what your CAO will be for the next call on this customer? ____ ____
- Did you update your customer record? ____ ____

Index

Note: An *n*. after a page number refers to a note; an *f*. refers to a figure.